P9-CCZ-657

Journal Types for Your Specific Needs

The Log Journal (Chapter 6)
➤ Keep a record of contemporary life.
➤ Create a detailed record of events for future reference.
➤ Set goals and work toward those goals.
➤ Keep track of diet and exercise routines.

The Healing Journal (Chapter 7)
➤ Manage pain.
➤ Keep track of symptoms.
➤ Maintain a positive frame of mind.
➤ Track your medication.

The Cathartic Journal (Chapter 8)
➤ Vent your emotions.
➤ Tell your side of the story.
➤ Say everything you wish to say about a subject.
➤ Record what you wish you had said or done in the past.

The Unsent Letter (Chapter 9)
➤ Say good-bye.
➤ Say things you should have said to a particular person.
➤ Express regret.
➤ Express other emotions.
➤ Tell someone you miss him or her.

The Theme Journal (Chapter 10)
➤ Plan a special event.
➤ Record weeks or months of a continuing activity.

The Reflective Journal (Chapter 11)
➤ Explore your character.
➤ Improve your character.
➤ Explore and expand your code of ethics.

The Spiritual Journal (Chapter 12)
➤ Explore the state of your soul.
➤ Explore your relationship with God.
➤ Achieve peace of mind.
➤ Strive toward a better relationship with God.

The Family Journal (Chapter 13)
➤ Record family events.
➤ Chronicle family growth.
➤ Chronicle children's growth.
➤ Record special family events.

continues

tear here

alpha
books

Journal Types for Your Specific Needs   (continued)

The Dream Journal (Chapter 14)
- ➤ Record dreams.
- ➤ Analyze dreams.
- ➤ Make decisions based on what your subconscious mind is trying to tell you.

The Historical Journal (Chapter 15)
- ➤ Record events of the past.
- ➤ Get a sense of your accomplishments.
- ➤ Compare the past with the present.
- ➤ Make sure you have certain things written down.

The Travel Journal (Chapter 16)
- ➤ Keep track of mileage and expenses.
- ➤ Record all the places you went.
- ➤ Write about people you met.
- ➤ Remember impressions.

The Hobby Journal (Chapter 16)
- ➤ Record why this hobby interests you.
- ➤ Discuss how you got started.
- ➤ Describe projects.
- ➤ Keep track of your increasing skills.

The Writer's Journal (Chapter 16)
- ➤ Record ideas.
- ➤ Save great lines.
- ➤ Archive project beginnings.
- ➤ Develop characters.
- ➤ Record ideas.

How to Strengthen Your Writing

- ➤ Write in the active voice.
- ➤ Use active, past-tense verbs.
- ➤ Use adjectives and adverbs sparingly.
- ➤ Choose your words carefully.
- ➤ Avoid using the same word repeatedly.

Three Rules for Constructing Plot

- ➤ **Tell 'em what you're gonna tell 'em.** Introduce your subject.
- ➤ **Tell 'em.** Develop your subject.
- ➤ **Tell 'em what you told 'em.** Review your subject matter.

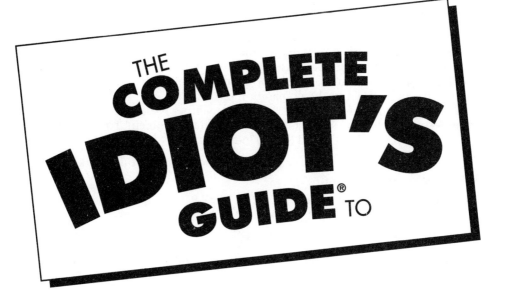

THE COMPLETE IDIOT'S GUIDE® TO

Journaling

by Joan R. Neubauer

alpha
books

Macmillan USA, Inc.
201 West 103rd Street
Indianapolis, IN 46290

A Pearson Education Company

International Standard Book Number: 0-02-863980-4
Library of Congress Catalog Card Number: Available upon request.

03 02 01   8 7 6 5 4 3 2 1

Interpretation of the printing code: The rightmost number of the first series of numbers is the year of the book's printing; the rightmost number of the second series of numbers is the number of the book's printing. For example, a printing code of 01-1 shows that the first printing occurred in 2001.

Printed in the United States of America

Note: This publication contains the opinions and ideas of its author. It is intended to provide helpful and informative material on the subject matter covered. It is sold with the understanding that the author and publisher are not engaged in rendering professional services in the book. If the reader requires personal assistance or advice, a competent professional should be consulted.

The author and publisher specifically disclaim any responsibility for any liability, loss, or risk, personal or otherwise, which is incurred as a consequence, directly or indirectly, of the use and application of any of the contents of this book.

Publisher
Marie Butler-Knight

Product Manager
Phil Kitchel

Managing Editor
Cari Luna

Senior Acquisitions Editor
Randy Ladenheim-Gil

Development Editor
Jennifer Moore

Senior Production Editor
Christy Wagner

Copy Editor
Amy Lepore

Illustrator
Jody Schaeffer

Cover Designers
Mike Freeland
Kevin Spear

Book Designers
Scott Cook and Amy Adams of DesignLab

Indexer
Amy Lawrence

Layout/Proofreading
Angela Calvert
John Etchison

Contents at a Glance

Contents

Foreword

Journal writing for personal growth, creative expression, and life documentation has come a long way since our ancestors drew pictures on cave walls. In the last quarter-century, reflective writing has evolved into a genuine movement. And with the publication of *The Complete Idiot's Guide to Journaling,* the joys and comforts of the journal come alive for another generation of writers.

Standing on the broad shoulders of the journal classics—Ira Progoff's *At a Journal Workshop,* Tristine Rainer's *The New Diary,* Christina Baldwin's *Life's Companion,* and my own *Journal to the Self*—Joan Neubauer offers up a smorgasbord of helpful hints, fun facts, and timeless strategies for exploration and self-knowledge. But she doesn't stop there. A quick glance down the table of contents shows a remarkable and refreshing breadth: You can write journals to celebrate the new or memorialize the old, for healing or for history, on a computer or in a blank book, to keep track of bright ideas or to log the little pleasures of life. Stretching beyond the trilogy of mind/body/spirit, *The Complete Idiot's Guide to Journaling* also cleverly coaches readers/writers on ways to keep the writing itself fresh and interesting, and how to plug into the online journal revolution.

I am a journal therapist and have spent a career studying with relentless curiosity how writing heals. The single most frequent question I am asked is, "How do I get started?" This useful guide answers that question dozens of times over, blending classic wisdom with common sense in an upbeat, energetic style. Whether you are a novice or an experienced writer, *The Complete Idiot's Guide to Journaling* will be a welcome addition to your self-help library and will stimulate many absorbing hours writing the books of your own life.

Kathleen Adams LPC, RPT

Kathleen Adams LPC, RPT, is a Registered Poetry/Journal Therapist; Director, The Center for Journal Therapy (www.journaltherapy.com); and author of *Journal to the Self* and *The Write Way to Wellness.*

Introduction

Your life has great meaning, and you have the power to make things happen. You draw upon that power to deal with life's everyday inconveniences as well as its darker tragedies. Imagine what you could accomplish if you could tap into that strength at will. Keeping a journal can guide you to realize the potential of that power.

A very powerful tool, your journal gives you the time and space to reflect upon your life, take joy in it, find your place in the world, take control, and succeed. I know, that sounds like a tall order for something as simple as a journal. But remember, you are the driving force, not the journal. The journal merely provides the vehicle for you.

When you begin to write, let yourself feel the magic flow through you to the words on the paper. Let your mind explore the deepest corners of your soul. Let the feeling empower you to become the person you were meant to be.

In this book, I hope you will find many ways to use this very powerful tool—your journal—to your best advantage and to convince you that you can do anything.

How This Book Is Organized

This is a big book with a lot of useful, practical information about journals as well as some theory for you to use in developing your own brand of journal. You'll notice that there are five parts, each one exploring a different aspect of journal writing. Taken as a whole, they will guide you through beginning, developing, and maintaining a satisfying and productive journal for yourself and generations to come.

Part 1, "Exploring the Journal," gives a brief description of journal history, the basics of getting started, and scheduling a regular time and place for your journaling.

Part 2, "Pick a Journal, Any Journal," guides you through the various kinds of journals and their specific purposes.

Part 3, "What to Write, What to Write," gives suggestions on the kinds of things you might like to include in your journal.

Part 4, "How to Write," offers lessons for strengthening your writing style, using your computer for journaling, and taking advantage of program features to improve your writing.

Part 5, "Taking Control with Your Journal," brings all the lessons of the book together for a final review and offers suggestions for taking control of your life and formulating a philosophy of life using your journal.

The Appendix offers a list of suggested sites to aid in your use of the Internet in this lifelong pursuit.

Extras

You'll find a number of sidebars scattered throughout the book that will give you special tips, advice, and quotes.

Words of Wisdom

These boxes contain quotes from a variety of sources that I hope will inspire and instruct.

The Write Idea

These offer you additional information that you can use for recording in your journal.

Putting Pen to Paper

These are tips to help get you started journaling.

Trademarks

All terms mentioned in this book that are known to be or are suspected of being trademarks or service marks have been appropriately capitalized. Alpha Books and Macmillan USA, Inc., cannot attest to the accuracy of this information. Use of a term in this book should not be regarded as affecting the validity of any trademark or service mark.

Part 1
Exploring the Journal

Dear Diary,

Tomorrow is the first day of school. I hope I don't wake up with a pimple in the middle of my forehead. I need to make a good impression.

Go ahead and laugh. I know too many among us who can relate to this diary entry. After all, most of us kept diaries back in the days when dances and the opposite sex dominated our thoughts, and those are the sorts of things we wrote about.

Now, in a more mature stage of life, you've decided to keep a journal again, to keep a contemporary account of your life. But I warn you, keeping a journal can be habit-forming. One day, you'll wake up and realize you have reaped benefits you never dreamed of.

Journals—a Quick and Dirty History

We all think about our legacy, but the shape each legacy takes is different for everyone. Many people consider their children and grandchildren as their legacy and thus focus much of their energy on raising the best family they can. Others see their legacy in their professional lives, devoting endless hours to their careers. Many selfless people consider their bequest to the future as the work they do to help those in need—whether spiritually, economically, or emotionally. We all want something of ourselves to continue after we're gone, and journals provide a great way to help us leave concrete evidence of our existence. For many people, the journals become like a treasure trove of experiences and lessons, and after they die, those left behind view them as treasured mementos, a legacy far more valuable than gold.

A journal, on its simplest level, provides a home for our memories. If written from the heart and with a purpose, however, it becomes the vehicle that takes part of us—our heart, soul, and emotions—into the future.

Through our journals, we learn about ourselves and, in turn, leave those lessons for the future. As has always been the case with our species, the wise among us look to the past, learn from it, and step more confidently into the future.

With that in mind, let us look to the past to learn something more of this marvelous tool called a journal.

Caves, Clans, and Campfires

As a student of history, I find our ancestors a constant source of amazement. Granted, they didn't have the advantages of our advanced technology. Their study of the world around them was shrouded in superstition and lacked the sophistication of scientific method. Nevertheless, they were keen observers.

They studied birds as they flew and predators as they stalked their prey. They watched the great heroes of the clan and made mental notes of their exploits, hunting skills, and bravery against adversaries. From such observations came oral histories. Storytellers developed the characters into larger-than-life beings and embellished the stories. Mythologies developed and members of the clan, young and old alike, gathered around the campfire at night. They listened with rapt attention as their storytellers wove tales of heroism.

Words of Wisdom

"Whoso desireth to know what will be hereafter, let him think of what is past, for the world hath ever been in a circular revolution."

—Sir Walter Raleigh

In time, our ancestors developed a way to record these stories to share with others. Whether carved in stone or on pieces of bark, little symbols soon took on meaning, and with this meaning came a new authority. Writing something down gave it importance and worth.

With the advent of the written word, a whole new world opened to those who could master the skill. Stone and tree bark, terribly inconvenient from the beginning, eventually were replaced by paper, an invention that made it possible for more people to write about a wide variety of subjects.

Observers became the scribes who left us an incomparable eyewitness testimony of their time and place in the world. Among those scribes were the ancient Greeks, who laid the foundation for the modern journal.

Looking to the Stars

Great observers, the ancient Greeks looked at and tried to explain everything around them, below them, and above them. Early Greek astronomers in particular took great pains to observe the heavenly bodies, to accurately record their movement through the heavens, and to plot their paths through the cosmos. Over time, their daily logs, called ephides, made it possible for them to predict the behavior of the stars and planets from year to year. Their ephides also became the basis for future studies in astronomy and introduced the concept of a daily, running narrative—the journal.

An Idea Catches On

Once people had the tools—paper and ink—and the knowledge, they began recording all kinds of things. Of course, rulers liked the idea of a daily chronicle of their reign, but it didn't stop there. Doctors recorded information about their cases, particularly their "cures" and frustrations, as a way to pass on hard-earned knowledge to physicians who came after them.

Carpenters and architects kept scrolls of drawings in which they recorded new designs and the progress of long-running projects. A large structure might take 100 years to complete. It simply would not do for the architect to die without leaving a record behind to guide the next person on the job. Each generation of architects studied the drawings of those who went before, continued plans, modified them, improved upon them. Great new strides in the art and science of building great structures such as cathedrals were possible because of this marvelous means of passing on information. Without it, Notre Dame in Paris might not have the magnificent flying buttresses for which it is so renowned.

Merchants also kept daily records of transactions. They tracked expenses, income, and inventory to run their businesses more efficiently and profitably. Without such a system, we might never have the system of bookkeeping presently in place, or the banking system, or the stock market of today. The list goes on with each profession utilizing some type of journal for a different purpose, and each one took the idea to heart because it provided so many benefits. And then a new use for the journal came on the scene and, with it, a new articulation of what it meant to be human.

Putting Pen to Paper

Start observing people, places, and things around you more carefully. Then, for fun, try to predict the behavior of people you know or the outcome of events you witness.

From the Soul

St. Augustine of Hippo, born in A.D. 396, left us one of the best-known journals in the world. As a young man, he led a carefree life of easy money, easy women, lots of wine, and even more gambling. Then God touched his soul, and he changed his life dramatically.

Leaving his old life behind, he became a priest of the Catholic Church and rose to become bishop of Hippo, present-day Algeria. But the changes did not come easily. He struggled almost daily with temptation and strove for holiness. During that struggle, he learned much about himself and related the story of his spiritual awakening and development in his autobiographical journal called *Confessions*.

In *Confessions*, St. Augustine analyzed himself much as any modern-day psychiatrist would. Those who read his work have found the study of self to be fascinating, and it has become the basis for the reflective journal that so many of us find useful in our own lives.

The Write Idea

Perhaps the most famous pillow book, *Makura no Sōshi/The Pillow Book of Sei Shōnagon*, was written around the beginning of the tenth century. Full of mischievous reflections and anecdotes about court life, it is considered one of the masterpieces of Japanese literature.

The Write Idea

Samuel Pepys, an English diarist known for his diary, *The Diary of Samuel Pepys*, gave us an intimate look into England's upper-class life during the 1660s.

Pillow Talk

By the tenth century, the idea of journals and diaries had spread through the world like wildfire, even to the far reaches of Japan. The ladies of the Japanese court kept "pillow books," little notebooks they hid from the world under their pillows. In these diaries, they wrote about court gossip, of course, but they also recorded their innermost secrets, their hopes and dreams.

We don't know for certain why pillow books were so popular, but we can guess that, living in such a male-dominated environment, these journals gave the ladies of the court a means of self-expression. The diary would not judge them and would not spread gossip. They could write anything they wished within the pages of their book without fear of recrimination from anyone.

In the pillow books that still exist, we have an excellent source of information about the Japanese royal court and court life.

Royal Chroniclers

While the ladies of the Japanese court were reporting gossip, writing poetry, and delving into their souls, European royalty fell in love with the idea of recording the minutiae of their reign. They felt the world should know everything possible about them. They were, after all, leaving their mark on the world through their conquests and political intrigues. A chronicle would ensure that people would remember them and their exploits for a very long time. To achieve their immortality, they hired scribes who recorded everything: births, deaths, coronations, marriages, journeys, and edicts.

The Middle Class Rises

During the Middle Ages, a new economic class rose from the ashes of feudalism. Merchants, craftsmen, physicians, and scholars developed into this new thing called a middle class. Wealthier and better educated than generations before, more among them learned the art of writing, and they put this marvelous new skill to use as each profession and trade developed a new type of journal.

Like their counterparts in Japan, women of the Western world began keeping journals, such as the one penned by Margery Kemp (1373–1440), a lady of the middle class. An earthy tome, the author set down on paper a complaint about local churchmen for their treatment of her. I wonder if Geoffrey Chaucer knew Margery. She would have been the perfect model for the Wife of Bath in his *Canterbury Tales.*

A High Art

Journaling continued to grow in popularity right up to the Victorians in the nineteenth century, who raised the concept to a high art. Every well-born young lady and gentleman was expected to keep a journal as a vehicle for self-examination.

Within the pages of expensive, leather-bound volumes, young women and men of gentle breeding wrote their deepest secrets. In an age that valued self-control and a tight reign on emotions, those who kept a journal found a safe haven for self-expression.

Dear Diary

By the 1950s, nearly every teenage girl in America kept a diary. You know the kind I'm talking about. In fact, you probably had one. I sure did—one of those little books with a lock that could be used to keep nosy siblings from peeking.

If you went back now to review the entries, you'd probably laugh out loud at the things you wrote. Even though that new boy at school didn't talk to you, the sun still came up the next morning, and the earth still turned on its axis. But then, most teenage girls grew up and forgot about their diaries.

The Write Idea

French philosopher and mathematician Blaise Pascal (1623–1662) is known as the inventor of an adding machine as well as the developer of the modern theory of probability. He made extensive use of his journals to think through his concepts and work his theories, and design his mechanisms. Check out his book *Mind on Fire: A Faith for the Skeptical and Indifferent,* for insight into Pascal's mind.

Words of Wisdom

"Each human life has the potentiality of becoming an art work."
—Ira Progoff

The Father of Modern Journaling

During the same time that teenage girls were pouring their hearts and souls into their diaries, Dr. Ira Progoff, a renowned psychotherapist, asked some of his patients to do the same thing as an experiment. He encouraged them to keep journals as a way to achieve personal growth and to work through some of their problems. He called these journals "psychological workbooks," and he wanted his patients to record anything that came to mind, describe their emotional state, and report whether they felt something was missing in their lives. The important thing, Dr. Progoff felt, was to put their thoughts down on paper.

The Write Idea

Progroff left behind the rich legacy of his journaling method in his books, most notably *Writing to Access the Power of the Unconscious and Evoke Creative Ability*, which was published in 1992.

Shunning the traditional model of diagnosis and analysis, he instead focused on the spiritual and creative potential within the individual. He believed in journals as a very powerful tool and established the intensive journal method that he taught to nearly 200,000 people before he died in 1998 at age 76.

History's Lessons

As we look to the past, we find that famous and not-so-famous people kept journals for a variety of reasons, from counting money to taking account of their souls. Each found a reason to keep a journal. Each fulfilled a particular need. Each often found the benefit he or she sought.

Journals, nearly as old as the art of writing, can work their magic now, in the twenty-first century, if we look to the lessons of the past for empowerment, healing, growth, and success.

The Write Idea

Many years from now, your journals can give future generations an understanding of your time and place as no other resource can. You will become more than just a name and a date on somebody's family tree.

Putting Your Journal to Work for You

With the lessons of the past in mind, we know that there are no hard-and-fast rules for keeping a journal. Yes, there are some basic types. Yes, there are some basic techniques. But ultimately, you decide what kind of journal you wish to keep and what you wish to accomplish. You decide what works best for you to preserve the events and treasures of your life on paper.

Come with me now as we begin the exciting adventure into your future, through the pages of your journal.

The Least You Need to Know

➤ When we keep a journal, we contribute to our legacy.

➤ The history of journals can be traced back nearly to the dawn of writing.

➤ People have used journals to record activities, keep accounts, explore their souls, and try out new ideas.

➤ Once you learn about the many kinds of journals, you can choose the kind that works best for you.

Chapter 2

Is Journaling the Thing for You?

In This Chapter

➤ Recognizing that every life is worth recording

➤ Seeing the potential benefits of journaling for children

➤ Journal-keeping as a perfect outlet for teenage angst

➤ It's never too late to start keeping a journal

That the sun always rises in the east is a basic fact about our world. That's the reality; however, as John Lennon once said, "Reality leaves a lot to the imagination." You know exactly what I mean, but let's explore the idea a bit more.

If you asked 10 people to watch the same sunrise and then asked them to describe the sun rising above the horizon, I guarantee that each person would provide a different account of the same physical event. Some people would emphasize the growing light, some the changing colors on the horizon, and still others the increasing warmth as the sun rose higher in the sky. They all saw the same sunrise, yet each perceived it differently.

From this example, we can see that we each bring to any event or experience our own set of ideas about its importance, our impressions of it, and our own particular way of describing it. Likewise, only you can write about the emotions you experience as your children celebrate each birthday or the feeling you get when someone special embraces you. Make no mistake, your story and mine, though both set in the late twentieth and early twenty-first centuries, will emerge as very different accounts of the times in which we live because each of us see things in very different ways.

Everyone Has a Story to Tell

Since each of us perceives life uniquely, we can each offer a distinct view of our life experiences, our hopes, our dreams, and our secrets. If you think about yourself in these terms, you take on a whole new importance, not only in your mind but also in the pages of your journal and subsequently—if you choose to share your journal with others—to future generations. Your experiences and your perceptions have value.

I have met people from all over the world in my memoir- and journal-writing workshops. After the presentation, I enjoy talking with the participants who very often stay afterward to visit. They often share their stories with me, regaling me with tales of their childhood, their families or careers, or their participation in some historic event. Everyone has a story to tell or a certain perspective of the world that is important and unique. Why not keep a record of these stories, ideas, and thoughts?

No matter your age or place in the world, you have a story worth telling, a story that day by day grows in detail and complexity. Whether you're 6 or 60, recording the events of your life will be an invaluable treasure for you to review in years to come. You'll be able to review how you and your life have changed, what mistakes you made, and what successes you enjoyed.

Words of Wisdom

"However, no two people see the external world in exactly the same way. To every separate person a thing is what he thinks it is—in other words, not a thing, but a think."

—Penelope Fitzgerald, *The Gate of Angels*

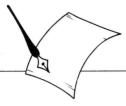

Putting Pen to Paper

Children love to explore and ask questions. When they learn something new, it gives them a feeling of accomplishment, and they want to put their new knowledge to use immediately. Take advantage of this curiosity and enthusiasm, not only for journal writing but also in all aspects of life. Teach. They will happily learn.

For the Children

It is never too early to present the idea of keeping a diary to a child. Along with a vivid imagination, children possess a great deal of curiosity about everyone and everything they encounter. This is nature's way of ensuring the learning process. Take advantage of that desire to explore, to discover, to know. Let children see you write in your journal each day. Allow them to share your enjoyment as you make your daily entries.

Children, even babies, often are smarter than we give them credit for and can immediately read someone's mood. When they see the joy you take from writing, the idea will intrigue them, and they'll ask you about it. Seize the moment and tell them exactly what you're doing.

Give them a simple explanation: "This is my journal, and it's like my best friend. I can tell it all my secrets. It makes me feel good to do that."

Children love the idea of secrets, and you can even ask your little knowledge seekers if they have any secrets of their own. Most likely, they'll say they do. Ask if they'll share their mystery with you. When they do, you have hit upon a golden moment.

The Golden Moment

The moment a child shares the treasure of a confidence, recognize it as a golden moment. After the child shares the information with you, say something like, "That would be a great thing to keep in a diary just like mine." Just watch their eyes light up. The idea of them keeping a diary just like you implies that you view them as a special friend, and they will jump at the chance.

Don't worry if you don't have an extra journal book on the shelf. Pull a sheet of paper from any notebook. Place the child's name at the top along with the date, and you have officially started the journal. In other words, strike while the iron is hot. Begin with the secret as the first entry and explain that you can write in the journal together every day. If the child doesn't know how to write just yet, have him or her dictate the entry to you.

Suggest that you go shopping together for the child's very own book to use as a diary. The prospect will thrill the child and will nurture his excitement for journal writing. Let the child choose the book.

Once home, begin the formal journal-keeping ritual. Set aside time each day to encourage the child to make entries in his book. Let him draw pictures or whatever he wishes to do on any given day. Let him express himself in a totally uninhibited way because, as he draws or scribbles "words" across the page, he will talk to you and describe exactly what he's "writing."

For a caring adult and a young child just beginning to keep a journal, this simple action of shopping together and writing in the journal will bring them closer and perhaps begin the child on a lifelong journey of journaling.

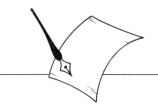

Putting Pen to Paper

If you know a child who might enjoy keeping a journal, buy an attractive book ahead of time. Keep it for when you encounter that golden moment or give it as a birthday or Christmas present. Inscribe the first blank page with encouraging words about keeping a journal. Sign it and date it. The child will always treasure that first diary, especially if you already have a wonderful relationship with the child.

The Write Idea

In many schools, journal-keeping is part of the regular language arts curriculum. Keeping a journal at home could prove advantageous to your child at school.

Growing Up

Once a child learns to read and write, the entire process of keeping a journal seems magical. Imagine, you can write things on paper that other people can read or that you can keep a secret from everyone. What a marvelous invention!

Of course, as their writing skills develop and as they write about more personal things, they'll want to keep their diary entries a secret. While respecting their privacy, you can still involve yourself in a creative way. Each day before the child begins to write, sit and talk with her about her day.

Ask which friends she saw and talked with. Ask about her teachers, homework, and what she's been learning about in school. Ask if anything exciting happened to her that day. The questions aid children in their review of the day and help them decide what to write about in their diary. And while they write in their journals, you can sit beside them and write in yours.

The Write Idea

Talking about the day's events and sharing journal time is an excellent way to establish and strengthen communication with a child. Such give and take between adult and child can lay a strong foundation for years to come.

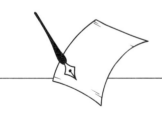

Putting Pen to Paper

Teenagers especially need someone to talk to. When they keep a journal, they use it not only as an outlet for their many feelings but as a means to gather the courage to find a trusted adult to talk to if the need arises.

The Case for Teens

The mantra of teenagers since the beginning of time has been, "No one understands me." You've said it. I've said it. We've all heard it more than once. Make no mistake—the teen years are difficult ones.

With hormones raging and physical and emotional changes rampant, they find themselves too old to be kids and not old enough to be adults. They hate the terms "young people" or "young adults." They chafe at authority and rules because they not only know better, they know it all. And yet they cry at the drop of a hat because of a parent's glare or a friend's snub. Lord knows I wouldn't want to relive those years, and I know few people who would.

Teens can fill a great void in their life with a journal. Teenagers who keep a diary say that writing helps them to sort things out and to see the true importance of events in retrospect. For a teenager, retrospect might only be a day or two, but even that short time period can be of value in seeing something in a more objective light.

Waking up in the morning to see that their face has broken out overnight can be an emotional experience for 15-year-olds. They dread the prospect of going to school and letting everyone see the imperfections. But three days later, when the blemishes have begun to disappear, they realize it wasn't as bad as it seemed at first. Writing about these things in a journal can help them gain the perspective they need to deal with the larger events life will cast in their direction.

Probably the best way to encourage teens to keep a journal is to buy them a stylish notebook and pen (or some hot new journaling software if they have a computer) and let them decide how to proceed from there.

The Write Idea

Researchers tell us that, contrary to past beliefs, learning can and does continue until the day we die.

For Adults Only

"You can't teach an old dog new tricks."

Wrong. Don't you believe it.

Don't think that, if you didn't start to keep a journal as a child, you've missed the boat. No one ever wrote such a rule, and you can jump in at any time. In fact, many people I talk to didn't begin until they were into their thirties or forties. Some didn't feel the need until their retirement years.

My advice: Start as soon as you can. Don't fret about how to write, when to write, or what to write. We'll discuss all these questions in future chapters. Truthfully, these points fade in comparison to the actual writing. The important thing is that you decide to keep a running narrative of your life, make the commitment, and do it. Write about whatever comes to mind, but write.

Fulfill the Need

"No one is perfect."

It might be trite, but it's also true. We all have flaws, and we all know of things about ourselves that we could improve. Perhaps we think we should be more generous, spend more time with our family and friends, be more reflective, or find a more satisfying career. We may be disappointed in ourselves or our relationships. We may wish for better health or for a way to take control of our life.

"You can't fix something until you know that it's broken."

It's another trite expression, but again, a valuable one. No matter what you want to change about your life, I believe that, if you identify the problem or the goal, make a plan, and follow through on your plan, you can make the change or achieve the goal.

Keeping a journal allows you to do all of these things. By confiding in your journal, you can discover more about yourself and determine what you most want to change—you can find out what's "broken." You can then use your journal as a tool to "fix" that broken part of yourself—whether that means making more time for your family, learning a new hobby, becoming more generous, or getting out of debt.

No matter how old you are, no matter what your background is, and no matter how good of a writer you are, journaling allows you to keep a unique record of your life and to explore, reflect upon, and even improve that life. I invite you to continue reading this book to learn more about journals than you may ever have imagined.

The Least You Need to Know

➤ Journals allow us to keep a unique record of our unique lives.

➤ It's never too early to get a child started on a journal.

➤ The most important step is the first one: putting pen to paper!

➤ Keeping a journal can fulfill an important emotional need for kids, teens, and adults.

Begin at the Beginning

Making a commitment to keep a journal means being willing to form a habit. As when beginning any new routine, it might seem like a chore at first, but once you get into the groove, it becomes something you look forward to because it engenders so many good feelings on so many levels.

Athletes often describe the act of participating in their sport on a regular basis—whether running, dribbling a basketball, or swimming laps—as being "in the zone." Once you become accustomed to writing every day, you, too, will experience the zone. Your feelings of accomplishment will stay with you until the next day when you sit down to make another entry, and the beautiful cycle begins all over again.

The First Step

When you decide to keep a journal, you make the commitment to something more than just sitting down every day to write in a book. Depending on the type of journal you choose to keep, you commit to contemplating your life, recording your life story, exploring your spirituality, or working toward a goal. None of these commitments—or the many other things you can use your journal to achieve—are trivial. When you pick up a pen to write in your journal, you are creating new possibilities for yourself. I'd say that's something worth committing to!

Think carefully about making the commitment. Of course, I think you should give it a try, but make sure it's the right decision for you. Once you make the commitment, meet that commitment each day and see what happens.

Buy the Book

Think back to when you were a child and how you looked forward to the first day of school. As the days of summer waned, you waited for the day when you could pick out your school supplies—those colorful pens, folders, notebooks, and markers. I don't know about you, but I thought the longest and the hardest about what kind of notebook I wanted, making sure I picked one with the right color cover, the right kind of lines, the right thickness of paper. It's probably silly, but I just felt that having the right notebook would make all the upcoming writing and note-taking easier and more enjoyable.

In just the same way, when you choose your journal, you need to find a book—the "right" book with the perfect cover, color, paper, and lines—that invites you to share your thoughts and will make you look forward to writing every day.

Choices, Choices ...

If you like bright colors on the outside and white paper inside, I'm sure you can find a notebook to suit that desire. If you prefer pastel-colored paper with lines, you can find one like that, too. Take your time and have a little fun shopping for your journal. Bookstores and office-supply stores usually have the widest variety of books to choose from, so you might want to begin your search there.

Perhaps you'd like something simple with little or no decoration or something a bit more ornate with a quilted cover and scented pages. Whichever you choose, make certain you love the look and feel of it. Don't be afraid to touch it. Note the feel of it in your hand when you pick it up. Ask yourself, "Could I look forward to writing on these pages every day?"

Flip through the pages. Are they lined? If not, would you prefer that they be lined? Some people would rather have lined pages because they struggle to write on a level line. Others prefer unlined pages because they like to sketch and glue pictures onto their pages.

Words of Wisdom

"The longest journey begins with the first step."

—Confucius

The Write Idea

Journaling gives you the time you need to act as an observer of your own life. Seeing things from a distance often gives us the advantage of objectivity, and we can recognize concepts and things about ourselves we otherwise might have missed.

The kinds of books you'll find when you go shopping may surprise you. Let's discuss some of the more popular ones.

The Binder

Just looking at a three-ring binder brings back a flood of school memories, an experience I'm sure many people share. They find comfort in its familiarity, and for that reason alone, some people may choose such a book for their journal.

At any large office-supply store, you'll find them in a wide range of sizes and styles, from simple, heavy-cardboard binders covered in blue canvas to elaborately tooled leather covers. If you'd like to design a cover for your book, you can buy one with a plastic sleeve on the front. You can slip a cover of your own design into it to mark it entirely as your own.

People like three-ring binders because of one very big advantage: Once they fill the pages with their writing, they can remove them, archive them, and add a whole new set. They can refill the book with new pages and continue their journal. The outside remains the same, which provides a certain comfort level. Nothing changes but the pages inside.

Putting Pen to Paper

Whatever book you choose for your journal, make sure it has acid-free paper so it doesn't disintegrate over time.

The Spiral Notebook

If you find a three-ring notebook too large or cumbersome to use, you might consider a spiral notebook as an equally inexpensive alternative. Just like binders, they come in different sizes, from notebooks small enough to slip into your pocket or purse to the standard 8" × 11". While the smaller notebooks might have some appeal, you probably won't get very many days recorded in each one, and you'll accumulate many notebooks over a short period of time, so storage might become a problem. But if you'd rather have a small notebook, try it out. It might work well for you.

The Write Idea

Scrapbook stores are also gaining in popularity around the country. You can most often find them in malls. They also carry a large selection of journals, papers, binders, and other materials that you might find interesting and helpful.

Larger, thicker notebooks will most likely serve your purposes better. The larger pages will feel less confining, freeing your creativity. Over time, you'll also have fewer books to store.

Manuscript Books

One of the most popular ways to keep a journal is in a blank manuscript book. You can walk into nearly any bookstore, stationery store, or office-supply store and find manuscript books of all sizes, bindings, and colors. You'll find some spiral-bound, but by far the perfect-bound styles are the most popular.

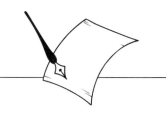

Putting Pen to Paper

Manuscript books provide a beautiful place to keep a journal. While a bit more expensive than other books, you can still find them for under $10, but the more expensive types can cost $50 or more. Some are refillable, but others are not, so be sure to take note of that before you decide which type you want.

The covers range from leather and velvet and brightly colored fabrics to quilted and laced. You can even buy beautiful covers into which you can slip less expensive manuscript books. When you fill the book, you remove it from the cover and replace it with another. From the great variety available, I'm sure you can find something to capture your imagination. Just like the diaries that secured all our teenage secrets, you can even find them with a tiny key lock.

As is the case with any journal, I encourage you to handle several before you buy. Pick them up. See how they feel. Compare them until you find one that feels right to you, one that makes your fingers just itch to start writing on those wonderful blank pages.

Don't fret over your decision about which style to choose. If at one time you pick a particular type of book and discover you'd rather have another, try a different style for your next volume. After all, variety adds spice to life. Using different types of journal books might spark a little extra creativity in your writing.

The Pen, or Pencil, or Marker, or ...

Okay, you get the idea. You need some sort of writing instrument to actually write in your journal. For the sake of convenience, I'll just assume that you like to write with pens and not, say, crayons. Because of the special job this pen will have, don't be afraid to spend a few extra dollars on it. You can find good quality pens nearly everywhere, from grocery stores to jewelry stores. Just find one that's right for you.

Take the time to handle the pen and take a "test write." Most places provide paper so customers can try out their pens before they buy. If you prefer a certain ink color, make sure the pen writes in that color and that you can buy refills.

Some people may consider this a trivial thing, but also keep in mind the thickness of your pen's point. Pens come in fine, medium, and heavy. As you try out the pens, take a good look at the lines they create. Ask yourself which one you would most like to write with. In fact, you might like two or three different thicknesses, especially if you like to sketch in your journal. They can each serve a purpose.

As with the book, make sure to use your pen only for writing or drawing in your journal. Don't carry it around with you to write checks or take notes at a business meeting. In addition to the fact that you could lose it, you should use it exclusively for writing in your diary. This exclusivity maintains its special purpose.

Exclusivity

By now you're probably wondering why it matters if you use your book or pen for things other than journal writing. It matters because keeping a journal should come to take on special meaning for you. Because writing in your journal helps you tap into the most hidden parts of yourself, that in itself serves a very singular function. When you pick up your pen to write in your journal, you shouldn't have to think about how you used that same pen to write a check at the grocery store. When you open your journal, you certainly don't want to see a note reminding you to call the plumber!

If you reserve your book and pen just for the purpose of keeping a journal, each time you make an entry, just opening the book and taking the pen in hand will be the only warm-up you need to write. Your brain will get right into gear, and you'll be off and running.

The Write Idea

At one time, only the rich could afford paper because it was so expensive. Today, however, it ranks among the least expensive commodities.

Tried and True

For thousands of years, people have recorded the day-to-day events of their life using the materials at hand, from tree bark to parchment to mass-produced sheets of white paper. Charcoal, goose quills, and ballpoint pens have been the instruments of expression.

For many people, the sensual experience of holding the book in their hands and smoothing the paper is part of the charm of keeping a diary. They'd be lost without the intimate contact with pen and paper and, in fact, might have no inclination to keep a journal without it. I like to remind people about the magic that William Shakespeare wove with nothing more than sheets of blank paper, ink, and a quill pen. Now it's time to cast your own enchantments.

The Digital Journal

For some people, writing with pen and paper is a silly exercise in this age of advanced technology. Instead, they find a boon companion in their computer with the thrill of tapping away on the keyboard. Don't agonize over it. Don't apologize for how you feel. You've chosen a different medium to perform the same task. All that matters is that it suits you and allows you to write every day. (If you don't plan to use a computer to keep your journal, you can skip the rest of this chapter and move on to Chapter 4, "The Journaling Habit." I'll see you there!)

Got Software?

You don't need fancy software to keep a journal on your computer. Any popular word-processing program will do just fine.

If you'd like specialized journaling software to help you, I suggest you do a little research to see if you can find a program you like. They each have some standard features like a time stamp and date of entry, but they also vary in small ways—so take your time. Some companies make free demonstration files available over the Internet, and you can download them to try them out.

The Write Idea

If you have Internet access, you might consider exchanging your journal entries with others over the Internet. With somewhere between 5,000 and 10,000 sites to choose from, you can discuss journals with others in chat rooms, make e-friends, and correspond with them on a regular basis. If keeping a diary is new to you, you might benefit from the encouragement others might send your way. They might even help you find a specific purpose for your journal and reap optimal benefits. See the appendix for some specific site suggestions.

If you decide on one of the popular word-processing programs, you essentially have a blank page to work with. I suggest you begin with a title at the top of the first page, identifying this as your diary. On the left-hand side of the page, add the date and then begin writing. If you are using journal-specific software, in most cases all you need do is fill in the blanks. Dates automatically appear, and some programs even suggest things for you to write about.

In either case, when you've finished your day's entry, save the file, and it'll be ready and waiting for you to add to it the next day.

You should, however, remember one thing if you're going to keep your journal on a computer. Keep a hard copy because, in 10 years, the newer computers may not be able to read files created today. In 20 years, computers may not even exist as we know them today. Although advances in technology may render your computer disks obsolete, a collection of printed pages can last for hundreds of years, whatever the technology. Just remember to print on acid-free paper.

The Choice Is Yours

Book or computer, pen or keyboard, the choice is yours, but don't stress over it. You always have the option to change your mind. Pick a different style of book. Choose another pen. Change your computer program. Whatever you select, however, it should meet your individual requirements and satisfy your needs.

Consider your comfort level and the very special nature of this endeavor. As you write in your journal day after day, you will be delving into some very personal places, perhaps territory you have never visited before. That's the important part. Express yourself by whatever means you choose and start today!

Putting Pen to Paper

Always make a backup copy of your work. A hard-drive crash could occur at any time.

The Least You Need to Know

➤ The most important step to journaling is the first one: Start writing!

➤ Writing in your journal every day will become a habit that will give you pleasure long after the activity is over.

➤ Take the time to choose the book and pen that are right for you.

➤ Consider using your computer to keep your journal.

Chapter 4

The Journaling Habit

In This Chapter

➤ Making a habit of journaling

➤ Choosing a time and place to write in your journal

➤ Starting out with five minutes a day

➤ Recognizing—and encouraging—your creativity

Quick! How do you put on your shoes and socks? Okay, you can stop laughing now. Really, think about it. Do you put on both socks and then both shoes? Or do you put on the left sock and then the left shoe, followed by the right sock and right shoe? Obviously, there is no right or wrong way as long as you end up with your shoes on over your socks. The order in which you accomplish this feat (excuse the pun) has come about because of habit.

Psychologists tell us that, if we do something every day for a period of 30 days, we form a habit. Journal writing, too, is a habit, one born of consistency of time and place and tool.

If you take a little time and make a little effort, you can form a habit that will serve you well in many ways throughout your life. In this chapter, I'll show you what you can do to start forming the habit of keeping a journal.

Your First Habits

Think back to your childhood and a time when your parents tried to teach you the importance of brushing your teeth after meals and before you went to bed each night. They probably had to remind you to perform the ritual for years before you did it automatically, just because you were a kid and that's how kids are.

"Don't go to school until you've brushed your teeth."

"Don't go to bed until you've brushed your teeth."

"Where do you think you're going? Into the bathroom and brush your teeth."

Finally, you got the idea, and if occasionally you found yourself flopping into bed in an exhausted state without brushing your teeth, you couldn't rest. Immediately, your parents' voices echoed in your mind, admonishing you to go to bed with clean teeth.

Despite all your attempts to clamp your eyes shut and fall asleep, you couldn't until you gave into the prodding of your conscience. Only when you had properly done your job could you go back to bed and fall asleep. Your parents did their job well. They pushed you kicking and screaming into forming an important habit. Now it's up to you to form another lifelong habit, that of keeping a daily journal.

Nag, Nag, Nag

If you give the process I'm going to propose in this chapter a chance, you can develop a journal-keeping habit that will stick with you for the rest of your life, reminding you to write each day in your journal. If you go to bed without writing in your journal, you may not be able to get to sleep because of the pangs of guilt. Of course, you can remedy the situation by getting out of bed and making your daily entry. But you don't have to let it go that far.

Forget that you don't have the time. Make the time. Forget that you don't have a book. Buy a book. Forget that you have a hard time remembering to do this. Form the habit. Don't even mention that you don't have the energy. That just won't fly. This isn't rocket science, and it doesn't require hours of your time. You can do this.

Easy Does It

Start easy. Set aside just five minutes every day to write.

When five minutes becomes easy for you, expand your time to seven minutes, and then to ten minutes. Before you know it, you may become so engrossed by the writing that you'll be doing it for thirty minutes before you realize how much time has passed.

Making the Time

More than any generation before us, we find our days filled with all sorts of responsibilities—from business presentations to PTA meetings. Car pools and job-site visits keep us on the road, and of course, don't forget the dry cleaners, post office, bank, and grocery store. We hardly have time to eat or give the kids a hug before we fall exhausted into bed at the end of the day.

Wherever we go, we have our cell phone in one hand and our day runner in the other, so it hardly surprises me when people say, "I'd love to keep a journal, but I just don't have the time." But just as we manage to find the time to brush our teeth twice a day, we can also eke out the time to keep a journal. You don't have to set aside hours, just a few minutes a day.

Putting Pen to Paper

Think of your journal as a daily responsibility to yourself.

Because you're trying to form the habit of writing in your journal every day, it's important to keep your start time the same day after day. This consistency will condition your mind to the writing and will help you establish and maintain the habit. You'll also find that the regularity will help your brain kick into gear.

You know yourself and your schedule better than anybody else, but I'm going to give you some suggestions and offer some advice that will help you find the time in your schedule that works best for you.

Words of Wisdom

In 1747, Lord Chesterfield, an English statesman, wrote a letter to his son addressing the use of his time. He wrote, "I recommend to you to take care of the minutes; for hours will take care of themselves." The same holds true for your journal. If you write a few minutes here, a page or two there, the daily exercise will produce volumes over a lifetime.

In choosing a time of day, take into consideration when you're least likely to be disturbed. You know this better than anyone. It's hard to do anything for yourself with the phone ringing, the boss demanding more, the pot boiling over, or the kids tugging at your pant leg. Here are some suggestions for how you can squeeze five minutes out of your day to write in your journal:

➤ Try getting up five minutes earlier in the morning or just head for bed a few minutes earlier than usual.

➤ Instead of spending all your time reading the morning paper at breakfast, set aside five minutes for your journal.

➤ If you have a 15-minute break at work in the morning and afternoon, you could take 5 minutes exclusively for journal writing.

➤ While waiting for the kids to get out of school, or waiting in any waiting room, you could take five minutes for your journal.

➤ Once you've got dinner in the oven and everything else under control, take a few minutes of the quiet time for yourself and your journal.

➤ After dinner, things sometimes settle down even around the busiest households. That might be a good time for you to make your journal entry.

➤ Once everyone else in the house is in bed and everything is quiet, that might be your best time for journal writing.

Putting Pen to Paper

In one of my workshops, a gentleman told me that, because he works different shifts on a rotating basis, he finds a regular journaling time difficult to adhere to. Instead, he ties his journal-writing time to his shower. If he takes a morning shower, he writes in his journal first, then showers, and then gets on with his day with the feeling that he's already accomplished something. If he showers at night, he showers first, then writes in his journal and goes to bed with a feeling of completeness. Either way, he feels like a winner.

Go on, do it! Give yourself permission to find time for yourself each day. Take a moment to close your eyes, kick off your shoes, and put your feet up, if only for five minutes. Look around you. Hug your kids. Listen to music. Smell the roses. *And write in your journal.* You can only do it if you slow down long enough to catch your breath and add yourself to your list of responsibilities and priorities.

What Part of Five Don't You Understand?

Please don't tell me you don't have as little as five minutes to spare each day. You spend more time than that deciding whether to have the number one or the number three at your favorite fast-food drive-through. The fact that you're reading this book tells me that you want to keep a journal. I'm just going to help you find the time.

Let's try a little exercise. I want you to set a timer for five minutes and then sit quietly. Don't do anything. Just sit and watch whatever's going on around you. Twiddle your thumbs or tap your foot if you have to, but don't do anything productive.

Putting Pen to Paper

Consider using your knowledge of your biorhythms to help you pick the best time of day to write in your journal. While outside influences affect us, our biorhythms have been pretty much set for us by our genes and millions of years of evolution. Morning people really do wake up feeling livelier. Night owls experience bursts of energy later in the day. A short and popular guide to learn more about your biological rhythms is *Biorhythms: A Step-by-Step Guide* by Peter West.

Tick, tick, tick …. The minutes drag by, don't they? It seems like an interminably long time and yet you didn't do anything.

Just think what you could have written in those five minutes about your feelings, your day, and the people in your life. You probably already started thinking about such things! I'll guarantee you, if you take that time to write, the minutes will fly by. Don't worry about what to write at this point. Gossip if you must, rant and rave about the poor service at the last restaurant you patronized, but write.

A Daily Dose of Writing

Ideally, you should write in your journal every day. The daily routine will condition you and increase your enthusiasm as your writing time nears each day. Your habit of writing at the same time each and every day will also make it easier for you to get into the proper mindset to write about the day's events.

In fact, the daily exercise will keep journal writing at the forefront of your mind, and you'll think about it often throughout the day. You might even make mental notes about points you'd like to include in your entry. With so much going on in your brain all day, you shouldn't suffer from writer's block. If anything, you'll have a wealth of material to choose from. If you do suffer from writer's block, however, I'll give you some tips in Chapter 16, "Other Types of Journals," to get you writing in no time.

Serendipitously, you'll also notice a rapid improvement in your writing skills. After all, you'll be practicing every day, and all skills (except maybe riding a bike) diminish without practice. Learning how to craft words to capture events and emotions with accuracy and verve comes with time and practice.

OUACHITA TECHNICAL COLLEGE

Reality Bites

Okay, let's face it. We all lead very busy lives, and sometimes our schedule is such that we can't possibly find or make the time every day to write in our journals. If you're one of those unlucky souls, perhaps another schedule would suit you. You have the ability to devise a schedule that meets your particular needs.

A woman I met at one of my journal-writing workshops said, "I have four kids, a husband, a full-time job, and a house to care for, and I still keep a journal. I take an hour every Sunday afternoon for myself, and part of that time includes writing in my journal. I just catch up on what happened the whole week before."

Putting Pen to Paper

Making an appointment with yourself gives you more control of your time, not only for journal writing but for anything else you want to do.

If this woman, with all her responsibilities, can make the time to write in her journal once a week, then anyone can. It only takes a little imagination to shift things around to fit your lifestyle. Look carefully at your responsibilities and carve out a few minutes for yourself.

Even if you keep a weekly or otherwise semiregular journal schedule, start out with only a few minutes, not a lot of time. The sense of achievement may surprise you and will become its own motivation to keep you wanting to write. You may enjoy it so much that you'll find more time for yourself during the week. Whatever schedule you design for yourself, mark it on your calendar to remind yourself, just as you would for any other appointment. Make this appointment with yourself and keep it.

Your Place or Mine?

Where you choose to write in your journal is as important as *when* and requires careful consideration. Confess. Does your appetite kick in the moment you walk into the kitchen? Of course it does. It happens to all of us. We respond this way because experience has conditioned us to expect good food in this place. Similarly, entering the space in which you choose to write in your journal will eventually elicit the desire to … you guessed it—write!

Maybe you have a particular spot—a nook in the attic or a desk in a study—in mind already, but if not, here are some ideas to get those creative juices flowing:

➤ In a corner of your bedroom

➤ Under a shade tree in your backyard

➤ At the kitchen table after the kids go to bed

➤ Just outside your front door watching the world go by

➤ At a favorite window

➤ In your bedroom or bathroom with the door locked

➤ At the Laundromat while you do your laundry

As you can see, you only need to use your imagination for places in which to keep your journal. But remember, it should be easily accessible and someplace you frequent on a regular basis.

Journal writing is a habit to which we condition ourselves. If at a certain time of the day, at a certain place, you sit down to write in your journal, you respond. Your body gets ready to write. Your mind sorts through the day's events, and your emotions kick into gear. It's all a matter of conditioning yourself. You can do this.

The Write Idea

You can condition yourself to any behavior by doing it at the same time, in the same place, and in the same way every day for 30 days.

Positive Reinforcement

Once you form the habit of writing in your journal at a regular time and place, keep it up. Don't lay off for a day or two, thinking it doesn't matter, because it does. It's hard work to form a habit, and this is one you want to stick. Keep your appointment with yourself and write in your journal according to the schedule you've set up.

Keep the Excitement Alive

As you keep your journal from day to day, you'll be pleasantly surprised as you notice an improvement in your writing skills. You'll feel more comfortable putting words on paper and expressing yourself. As you become more comfortable with the process, you'll free up your mind to be more creative.

Suddenly you'll realize that not only can you do this, you can do it well! You'll notice an increase in your enthusiasm, which will spur even more creativity, which nurtures more enthusiasm …. Well, you get the picture. It's a wonderful cycle that feeds on itself. Write every day and let yourself experience the excitement.

The Least You Need to Know

➤ It only takes five minutes a day to begin cultivating the daily habit of keeping a journal.

➤ Sitting down in the same place every day to write conditions you to add to your journal.

➤ If your schedule makes it impossible for you to keep a daily journal, consider writing a weekly journal.

➤ Once you get into the habit of writing in your journal, the creative juices will flow.

Chapter 5

Which Tool Do I Need—an Overview of Journal Types

In This Chapter

➤ How your lifestyle can determine the right kind of journal for you

➤ Taking a quick personality quiz

➤ Using your journal to improve your quality of life

➤ Experimenting with journaling

Before we begin discussion of the different kinds of journals, I'd like to share a popular analogy with you. I have used it for many years in my presentations, and I'm sure other journaling specialists, such as Kathleen Adams, have done the same.

Look into any toolbox and you'll find it packed with things like hammers, screwdrivers, files, and wrenches. You'll find pliers of all types as well as the lone nail or lost screw from a long-forgotten project. Each implement serves a particular purpose, and the craftsman uses each for that intention. You wouldn't use a screwdriver to drive a nail into a wall. It might work if you had a very small nail and a very soft wall, but it wouldn't be the most efficient means of accomplishing your goal.

Just as tools vary in their design and function, so do journals, with each type serving a particular purpose and fulfilling a certain desire. The decision about what kind of journal you wish to keep lies entirely with you, but the best way to make up your mind is to acquaint yourself with different types of journals, what purpose they serve best, and how those purposes will help you fulfill your needs. In other words, you need to determine which tool you need for the job at hand.

In deciding which type of journal you'd like to keep, it's important to remember one thing: Nothing is written in stone. The decision you make today could change tomorrow, just as your goals, needs, and moods change. You won't have to go out and buy a whole new book, just adopt a new attitude.

In previous chapters, I've discussed the history of journaling, why journaling might be right for you, and how to get started, but I've only hinted at the types of journals a person can keep. In this chapter, I provide an overview of the many kinds of journals people can and do keep.

If you wish to explore any of the journal types in more depth, you can turn to the individual chapter devoted to that type to find out more. Or maybe you'll decide that you want to keep a hybrid of many journal types, in which case you may choose to read a number of the chapters in Part 2, "Pick a Journal, Any Journal." Either way, consider this chapter to be the sampler platter from which you can choose your main course. *Bon appetit!*

Your Path in Life

You have enough decisions to make in your life. Don't worry about this one. If you find that a particular type of journal doesn't work for you, you can always switch canoes in the middle of the stream. You must also remember that your life changes from time to time, and your needs change accordingly. So what serves a particular purpose for you today may have no relevance in six months. A lot can happen in that short a time.

The Write Idea

Some of the most famous people in history kept journals, and they have ranged from gossip column fodder to deeply reflective musings. They each served a purpose at the time of their writing for their author, and today they give us a marvelous insight into another place and time.

You could get married, have a baby, change jobs, retire, or begin a second career. You may have to deal with a financial reversal, a divorce, or the loss of a loved one. You could get the biggest promotion of your life, or you could win the lottery. Each big change in your life will necessarily transform you and those around you and will alter your needs and wants. As a result, the type of journal you keep at any given time will vary according to those needs.

When considering the type of journal you'd like to keep, take your lifestyle, personality, and what you'd like to accomplish with your diary into account. Remember, a journal isn't just something to write in about your life; it's also a very valuable tool that can empower you in a way you never imagined. To get you started, I'll discuss several different kinds of journals and why people use them.

The Cathartic Journal

I know there are times when you'd just love to say or do certain things, but when you consider the consequences you realize it just isn't worth it. Yet, the anger and frustration still fester and you "need to get it off your chest." A cathartic journal gives you the means to say what you wanted to say and describe what you really wanted to do.

A cathartic journal allows you to cleanse your emotions or release emotional tension. Such a release often leaves the person feeling refreshed and renewed.

For example, if you have an intense job that requires a great deal of concentration or if you live in a situation that engenders a lot of stress, you might opt for a journal that allows a means of escape in which you can express your feelings freely. A cathartic journal might suit your needs best. See Chapter 8, "The Cathartic Journal," for more on this kind of journal.

The Goal-Oriented Log

On the other hand, even if your job requires a great deal of your time and energy, you may absolutely love what you do. In fact, if you have plans for recognition and promotions, a log could be a very powerful tool in your hands.

Chapter 6, "The Log," gives more specific information, but this type of journal lends itself well to stating objectives and working out ways to achieve them.

> **The Write Idea**
>
> Just as when you take a trip you need a road map and itinerary, a log journal can act as your "road map" to help you reach your destination.

The Reflective Journal

If you find it difficult to sort through emotional issues, you can use your journal as a way to do so in a very unthreatening way. A reflective journal nurtures reflection, introspection, and problem solving to give you the very outlet you may need. Check out Chapter 11, "The Reflective Journal," if you want to learn more about this kind of journal.

The Unsent Letter

If you feel you have things to say to someone but aren't prepared or able to share your thoughts with him or her just yet (or ever), you may find a useful tool in the unsent letter. See Chapter 9, "The Unsent Letter," for more information on this type of self-expression and its uses.

The Theme Journal

Sometimes a certain activity or event in life seems to take over, such as planning a wedding, searching for a new job, or renovating a house. In those cases, you might find that a theme journal that chronicles all the planning, excitement, and anxiety a useful tool. It can help you maintain control of the situation as well as keep your emotional equilibrium.

The Spiritual Journal

Nearly 90 percent of the people in this country profess to a belief in a Supreme Being and the existence of the soul. Many search for ways to improve their relationship with their Creator and to develop their spirituality. Within the pages of their journal they can analyze their present state of spirituality and make plans for becoming a more spiritual person. If this is an interest of yours, you might find a spiritual journal the perfect place to record all your thoughts and feelings about your soul, your God, and how to grow closer to the divine.

Words of Wisdom

"Set your affection on things above, not on things on the earth."

—Colossians 3:2

The Family Journal

Of all the journals, I think the family journal is the most fun. The whole family, from the youngest members to the oldest, can participate in some way. It's a great way to keep the lines of communication open among all members of the family and to strengthen relationships. It also makes it possible in years to come to relive precious moments.

The Dream Journal

Some people believe that the best ideas are born in our dreams, that state where we have no inhibitions and only uncensored and raw emotions. Wishes and desires very often make themselves known while we dream, and the perceptive individual can take lessons from what their nightly images tell them.

The Historical Journal

The historical journal is for those who wish they had started keeping a journal years ago.

"If only I had written about my children when they were babies."

"If only I had kept a journal when I started this job."

Those and more are among the laments I hear in my journal-writing workshops. I tell people that it's never too late to begin. The historical journal gives you the opportunity to catch up on lost time and tell all the stories from your life that you wish to preserve for all time.

The Healing Journal

For those among us who suffer from chronic conditions and diseases, a healing journal is a marvelous tool. In clinical studies, scientists have demonstrated that those who keep a healing journal very often manifest a reduction in symptoms, need lower medication dosages, and could enjoy a higher quality of life.

A Journal for All Seasons

You'll likely find that the type of journal you prefer to keep changes with the cycles of your life. For example, if you've just moved to a new city and don't have any friends or family nearby to talk to or to cry on their shoulders, you may find a cathartic journal to be a suitable temporary substitute.

Eventually, of course, you'll make new friends and acquaintances—maybe even start a family. We know that a good relationship of any kind requires at least a little work. You may decide that you need a reflective journal to explore your feelings about your relationships, your uncertainties, doubts, confidences, and wishes. Or perhaps you need to write some unsent letters to allow yourself to work through emotions you are feeling toward others.

The Write Idea

Don't be afraid to change the style of journal you keep. Instead, look forward to it as an opportunity to expand your horizons and perceptions.

You get the idea. Next you might set your sights on a goal and decide that a goal-directed log is the way to go. Or you might wish to begin a narrative journal of your life. Whatever you decide, you have the tools at hand with your journal. Remember, you can always change the kind of journal you keep— for change is the very essence of life.

The Right Journal for Your Personality

Just as you consider your lifestyle at any given time in your choice of journals, your personality also determines what type of journal works best for you. Everyone has certain preferences, and only you can determine which type appeals to you most.

Blind Dates with Great Personality!

Raise your hand if you've ever been on a blind date. What was the first thing you asked your friend who tried to set you up? Be honest. Yes, you asked what the person looked like. I know you just loved it when your friend answered with something like, "He's got a great personality."

It makes you wonder if anyone has ever described you in that way. Come to think of it, how would you describe your personality? Don't shudder at the thought of analyzing yourself. This could be important in determining the journal you'd like to keep.

I've developed a few questions for you to think about to help you discover what personality type you are. Once you've answered a few questions about yourself, you will probably have an easier time figuring what kind of journal might be most appropriate for that personality type. Be honest with yourself but don't be brutal when you consider the answers.

Are you easygoing?

Do have a need to record precious memories?

If you answered "yes" to both questions, you might want to consider a log as a contemporary record of events in your life.

Are you a competitive person?

Do you want to grow your business?

Are you looking for promotions and recognition in the workplace?

Goal-oriented and competitive people often find that keeping a log that records their progress toward a particular achievement is a useful tool.

Do you suffer from a chronic disease or condition?

Do you feel the need to unburden yourself or to correct an impression that other people have about you or an event?

Do your emotions often get in the way of good relationships?

If you answered "yes" to these questions, you might want to consider keeping a healing journal.

Writing about the things that bother you, such as your hypertension or arthritis, can help you to cope better with your condition and measurably improve your life.

Do you typically harbor resentments?

Do you feel the need to unburden yourself or to correct an impression that other people have about you or an event?

Do you remember an event from years ago that still bothers you?

You can work through unresolved resentments and unburden yourself of long-ago events that still trouble you by keeping a cathartic journal.

Do you forgive and forget?

Do you have unfinished business with someone you haven't seen for years or who has died?

Do you have difficulty expressing your emotions?

Try writing some unsent letters if you need to "finish some business" with someone who either has died or with whom you no longer communicate for whatever reason. It's also a good way to practice communicating with loved ones.

Are you looking for a means of spiritual growth?

Do you have lessons you wish to leave for your children and grandchildren?

Do you have some particular knowledge that you'd like to pass along?

Do you have difficulty determining what is most important in your life?

If so, consider keeping a reflective or spiritual journal. As you write about your most private feelings and desires, each can serve to guide you toward becoming a better person more concerned with issues of character and conscience than with material items.

Do events seem to dominate your life for months or years at a time?

Do you recognize recurring themes in your life such as inappropriate choices in relationships, finances, or jobs?

If you want to focus on a particular event or work through something in your life (such as quitting smoking), you might find that a theme journal is the way to go.

The answers you give to these questions can help you determine certain aspects of your personality that perhaps you've never thought of and, in the process, can help you decide which type of journal would serve you best. Of course, this is a very short list of personality traits. I'm sure you can think of more, and when you read each chapter about specific journal types, the information you glean can help you make a better decision.

Never forget that your journal is a tool and, as such, can help you achieve and improve the quality of your life. But you have to have the right kind tool for the desired result. Don't try to use a hammer to saw through a board!

Using Your Journal as a Sounding Board

Your journal can help you identify the most important things in your life. Even if we know what our priorities should be, it's often difficult to rearrange our lives to put relationships, jobs, spirituality, and everything else that absorbs our time and thoughts in the order they belong. You have to determine the order, and you have to determine how to make it happen.

Look at your journal as the perfect sounding board for the changes you'd like to make in your life. Give yourself permission to express yourself without fear or reservations. Be honest. Note the good things about your life and record the things you'd like to change.

Different Strokes for Different Folks

Complicated creatures that we are, what works for one person may not work for another. You are the jury of one who will decide which type of journal serves you best.

But whichever you choose, give yourself—your emotions and your creativity—free rein.

Write. Draw. Sketch. Glue pictures and comics to your pages. Copy a poem or expression that touches your heart or has some significance to you. Make comments about the times in which you live. Relate a funny joke someone told you. Every bit of it is part of your life.

The Write Idea

Let your imagination guide your choices of what other things to add to the pages of your diary. The more detail, the more variety you include, the more complete picture you paint of yourself within the pages of your journal.

The Mad Scientist Lives!

Cartoons and bad horror movies have bequeathed a lasting impression of the mad scientist who, for the past 20 years, has been trying to take over the world. Clad in a rumpled white lab coat, the man with tape holding his glasses together bends over yet another experiment, carefully measuring the next ingredient to add to the mix.

He can barely contain his excitement as he realizes that, if this experiment succeeds, he'll rule supreme! Okay, stop laughing. These movies are fun to watch late on a Saturday night while you share a big bowl of popcorn with friends, but believe it or not, you can learn an important lesson from the guy in the movie: If at first you don't succeed, try, try again.

What Works for You

When you begin to keep your journal, I encourage you to write whatever comes to mind. You will become more comfortable with the idea of writing as you form the habit. After a few days or weeks, though, you should begin to define what exactly you want from your journal and should determine how to get there.

By this time, I know it sounds as though keeping a journal will solve all your problems, make you rich and successful, and turn you into a saint. Not exactly, but you do have the potential within yourself. You need the appropriate education, experience, and understanding to achieve it. Your journal can help you in your journey, allowing you to prioritize, plan, track your progress, and determine when you have succeeded. The power is within you.

The Least You Need to Know

➤ You can use your journal as a very powerful tool to accomplish great things in your life.

➤ Lifestyle and personality play an important role in determining what kind of journal you keep.

➤ A journal helps you achieve growth of all kinds.

➤ The type of journal you keep will change over time as your life changes.

➤ The power to grow lies within you. Keeping a journal helps you tap into that power.

Part 2

Pick a Journal, Any Journal

A journal is a journal is a journal. Right? Wrong! A variety of journals exist, and they all serve a particular purpose. I'd like to share some of the more popular journal types with you so you can pick and choose the one that appeals to you most, that you think you'd have the most fun with, or that would best fulfill your needs. Don't think that just because you choose one you'll be stuck with it forever. As your life and your needs change, your journal can adjust to help you get through the toughest times and teach you to take pleasure in the joys life has to offer.

The Log

In This Chapter

➤ Keeping a contemporary record

➤ Seeing the value in the goal-oriented log

➤ Following three simple steps to reaching your goal

➤ Putting the goal-oriented log to work for you

I'll bet you've wished upon a star more than once in your life. We all have dreams and wishes. Too often, though, we let go of them because the thought of the effort involved in making them come true overwhelms us. However, your log can help you break the big picture down into more manageable pieces so that your dreams seem more attainable. You just have to know your destination. If you're a goal-oriented, competitive person, a log may be just the thing you're looking for. And if you're someone who would just prefer a running record of your life, a log will serve your purpose as well.

Where Does This Bus Go?

Imagine getting ready for a vacation and having no idea where you're going. You wouldn't know what to pack or how you were traveling. Worst of all, how would you know when you reached your destination?

You wouldn't because you had no destination—no goal. What a colossal waste of time, effort, and money. The same holds true for life.

Humans experience life on so many levels, and we always hunger for something more, something bigger, something better. We want a better job, more money, a bigger house, a tranquil home, or inner peace. You can use your log to help you achieve the things you desire, no matter what they are. You can do so much more in life if you lay out a plan for yourself. A log is a perfect way to keep yourself on track.

We can accomplish anything if we have the desire and a plan, and the best place to begin that plan is in your journal. The solitude of the process allows you the time to sort out what you want and to determine a way to get there. You only need to believe that you can achieve your goal.

Words of Wisdom

"I have always thought that one man of tolerable abilities may work great changes, and accomplish great affairs among mankind, if he first forms a good plan, and, cutting off all amusements or other employments that would divert his attention, make the execution of that same plan his sole study and business."

—Benjamin Franklin

The Write Idea

For an excellent example of a log journal wherein the author relates events of his life as well as his goals, check out Benjamin Franklin's *Autobiography*.

No Rocket Science Here

Benjamin Franklin, a man graced with many talents, played an integral role in the birth of this nation, but he left an additional legacy of his many inventions and insights through his writing. During his long life, he was a printer, inventor, scientist, and statesman. He never considered himself a genius but rather a "man of tolerable abilities," yet he understood the value of goals and planning.

We, too, can take a lesson from Franklin and his life when we set our own goals. It only requires two things: that we know what we want and that it be attainable. For example, you might want to fly to Saturn, but at our present level of technology, it's doubtful that you'll ever get the chance, regardless of whatever plan you might put in place. On the other hand, losing 10 pounds in the next two months could be a very achievable goal given the proper plan and your willingness to adhere to it.

Here are some sample goals that you can use your log to help you achieve:

➤ Lose weight

➤ Get in shape

➤ Begin a new career

➤ Go back to school

➤ Learn and master a new hobby or sport

➤ Learn and master a new skill

➤ Write a book or a short story

➤ Take an expensive or exotic trip

➤ Buy a new car

➤ Relocate to another area of the country

These are only a fraction of the many goals you can work to achieve by using your log. We all have things we want to achieve, relationships we wish to nurture, or things we wish to buy. Like the little engine that could, we can do it, too. We all know people whom we call "overachievers," and we wonder how they do it all. Whether they know it or not, they, like Franklin, set goals, made plans, and followed through on them.

You can achieve your goals, too, but it doesn't happen by magic. No genie is going to appear to grant your wish. No little elves will come to your house in the middle of the night to finish the painting in your living room. It's all up to you. You can do this.

Getting Started

For keeping a log, you need to remember three very important words: Simple. Simple. Simple. When you begin, write your log like a chronicle of your day—where you went, what you did, and whom you met. I know this sounds totally uninspiring, but it's a great way to get started. During your first week of journaling, you might want to just work on getting into the habit. In the process, you might decide that you like this particular journal form so much that you want to stay with it for a while.

Despite its simplicity, never underestimate your log's value as a powerful tool. It can help you bring about some very important changes in your life, whether you want to lose weight and get into shape, save enough money to buy a house, or run a marathon. Whether you like to compete with others or with yourself, the log offers an opportunity to set goals and track your progress.

We often refer to *The New York Times* as America's "newspaper of record." That is, we consider *The Times* a witness to events of the day. Your log serves the same purpose. Each day as you make your entries, you record the things that happened to you on that day, the people you met, the places you went. Since it's impossible to write about everything that happened to you in a given day, the skill lies in picking the most appropriate events, the ones you feel best represent you and your day. When you begin using the journal to help you reach a goal, you can pick the events and activities related to your goal, but when you're getting started, it's best to keep it basic.

Time to Hit the Replay Button

When first deciding what to write about in your daily log, start by closing your eyes. Take a deep breath, then replay your day in your mind on fast forward, just as you would a movie in your VCR. During your review, pick the event that stands out most in your mind.

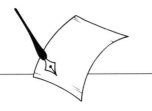

It could be the most dramatic, most emotional, happiest, or saddest event of the day; a first; or something funny that just about made you fall out of your chair with laughter. Then replay that single event more slowly. Take note of the people, the surroundings, and the action. Now take your pen in hand or fire up your computer and begin to write.

Include the people you interacted with, your conversations, and even specific dialogue if you can remember it. You might even include why this particular event stood out in your mind as it did, and then add one more thing—emotion.

The Sensual Log

Every schoolchild knows about the five senses: sight, sound, touch, taste, and smell. Since we experience life through our senses, the journal you keep should reflect those perceptions. So when you write in your daily log, try to include those descriptions. This will allow you to paint a more complete picture of the event or experience.

Putting Pen to Paper

Take care not to get bogged down in too much description. Include only as much as you need to set the scene—maybe two or three descriptions per paragraph. Unless the setting for the event is terribly unusual, such as dinner at the palace with the queen, don't dwell on it. Then start writing about the actual incident.

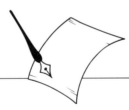

Putting Pen to Paper

Here's an example of sensory description in a journal entry:

> I walked into the waiting room with its plush champagne-colored carpet. The receptionist directed me to an overstuffed chair upholstered in deep burgundy brocade. As I waited, I listened to the soft classical music that came from the speaker in the far corner of the room.
>
> Before the first song was over, the receptionist came forward and said, "Ms. Jones will see you now." With much trepidation about what was to come, I followed her down the hall to the office. Along the way, I caught a whiff of roses from the bouquet perched on a nearby shelf.

From the preceding example, can you more clearly picture the incident? Surely it provides a richer description than something like, "I kept the appointment today with my attorney." You can do the same thing to bring any event or experience alive. Vivid, descriptive writing allows you to step right back into the scene when you read back through your journals, and it brings the event to life for any readers with whom you share your journal.

The View from Your Heart

While our senses give us the ability to perceive the world around us, our emotions allow us to react to it. Certain behaviors make us feel a certain way. When other people snub us or are kind to us, it elicits particular emotions in us. So each meeting and each action will bring out feelings in us.

If you decide to describe a meeting with a long-lost friend in your journal, describe how the meeting made you feel. Were you glad to see her? Did she have good news for you or relate something that caused you sadness? Whatever the incident, don't just describe it. Also describe the feelings it caused.

Writing your journal in such a way will paint a picture with your words, creating a more complete image of your experience. When you look back on what you've written, you'll more clearly remember it, and future readers will be able to put themselves in your shoes.

You can continue keeping your journal in this manner, making it a running narrative of your life, or move on to another concept with your log. You can add another dimension by using your log journal to help you achieve certain things in life.

Stating Your Goal

The concept of goals and plans can help you achieve a great deal in your life, and you can use your log to do it, if you so choose. How you do that is up to you, but let me give you a suggestion. Suppose you've decided that even though you like your job, you'd really like the position a level above the one you currently occupy. If you feel that you can realistically achieve that position, then that then becomes your stated goal.

Use your log to help you profit from life by setting goals and achieving them.

Words of Wisdom

"An empty book is like an infant's soul, in which anything may be written. It is capable of all things, but containeth nothing. I have a mind to fill this with profitable wonders."

—Thomas Traherne

When you define your goal, do it in three simple steps:

1. Make sure it is attainable.

2. State what you want to achieve.

3. Define your timeframe.

State your goal simply and in one sentence. For example, "I want to lose 10 pounds in the next two months." Write it in your log. Now you have the first line of your log.

Get Motivated

Once you've stated your goal, list the reasons why you want to reach it. Knowing your reasons for having the goal will help you maintain your motivation and will keep you on track. Real life often gets in the way of our best intentions. With all your responsibilities, you can easily get distracted from your goal.

Some common excuses people offer for not following through on their goals include fatigue, deciding the goal isn't worth pursuing after all, or not having enough time to devote to it. All of these excuses are valid, but they are, after all, just that—excuses. If you really want to achieve, if you want to succeed, you must never lose sight of your goal, and you must never forget your reasons for wanting it.

Putting Pen to Paper

If your goal is to write a book, you might have two reasons. Be sure to state them in your log. For example, you might write: (1) I have a good story to tell; and (2) it will provide information that people should know. I suggest that you even write your goal and your reasons on a separate piece of paper and tape it up where you will see it every day.

The Plan

With your goal clearly stated and your motivation foremost in your mind, the next step is to devise a plan that will help you get there.

You might not get it right the first time. That's okay. That's why you need to write in your journal every day.

Play with different plans. Set different courses of action. Experiment. Revise. Refine it until it looks right, until it feels right. Putting your plan on paper may take you a few days or weeks, depending on the complexity of your goal.

Again, once you come up with a plan that you like and that you think will work, simplify it. State it in a step-by-step manner. This technique will allow you to track your progress day by day in your log.

Work the Plan

At this point, you deserve a real pat on the back. You know where you're headed and what you need to do to get there—not many people do! Now comes the real work and real satisfaction.

Each day, as you write in your journal, remind yourself of your goal and your reasons for wanting it. Then ask yourself each day what you did to achieve that goal. Ask yourself if you accomplished any part, even the smallest bit, of your plan and then record your answer in your log.

Be honest with yourself and your journal. Take credit for the smallest successes. If, however, you didn't do anything to get yourself closer to your goal, record that as well and be sure to state the reason. Perhaps you got busy. Perhaps an emergency came up. That's okay. Life happens. But resolve to do better the next day. Try not to let a day go by without doing something to bring you closer to your goal.

Let's take the example of writing a book. The idea of writing an entire book could prove daunting for some. However, if you decide that each day you will write just one page, at the end of the year, you'll have a book consisting of 365 pages. And so it is with any aspiration. Don't look at it as a whole. Think of it as a series of small, bite-size steps that you can take one at a time.

After a short time, you'll begin to see your destination come into view, the light at the end of the tunnel, if you'd like. As you shorten the distance between you and your goal, your excitement will grow as well as your confidence and self-esteem, a trait that comes not so much from who we are as from what we do.

Words of Wisdom

"In preparing for battle I have always found that plans are useless, but planning is indispensable."

—Dwight D. Eisenhower

Goal!

Athletes of every sport feel a rush whenever they cross the finish line, get the ball in the goal, or outmaneuver their opponent. The surge of adrenaline and the feeling of a job well done are experiences like little else in this world. But you don't have to be an NFL athlete to enjoy the feeling. You, too, can experience the elation of attaining a long-awaited goal.

Words of Wisdom

"Ideals are like stars; you will not succeed in touching them with your hands. But like the seafaring man on the desert of waters, you choose them as your guides, and following them you will reach your destiny."

—Carl Schurz

You feel rightful pride in the accomplishment because you are the person who identified the goal. You devised a plan, and you are the one who worked the plan, day by day, step by step, to finally reach your destination.

Your log, much like a best friend, was there each step of the way with you, giving you the time and the space to work it all out in your mind and set it down on paper. Believe it or not, you encouraged yourself through your own words and will to never give up. At this point, you have to believe that you can do anything, given the right tools. For the attainment of goals, I can think of no better tool than the log.

Lose That Weight!

When I teach journal writing workshops, I talk about the importance and practicality of the log. Invariably, someone in the group asks, "So how can I use it to lose weight?" Let's kill two birds—losing weight and learning how to keep a goal-oriented log—with one stone in this section.

Of course, I always advise people to consult with their doctor when it comes to any matter of health, but let's assume your physician approves of you losing 10 pounds. You've already reached the first step: You've set a goal for yourself. Now state your goal in your log and give yourself a timeframe. Just for round numbers, and of course to make it easy, let's say you give yourself 10 weeks to lose 10 pounds, a pound a week. Is that doable? Of course it is. Write that down in your log.

With a little research and advice from your doctor, you can determine how many calories you can allow yourself each day to lose the weight. That, of course, will depend on your current age, weight, and activity level, but let's say for the sake of argument you have found that, at 1,500 calories a day, you can consume the necessary nutrients and still shed a pound a week. Write that in your diary as your plan.

The Write Idea

Keeping a log of your daily progress reinforces your behavior, keeps you on track, keeps your enthusiasm up, and brings you closer to your goal.

Each day thereafter, record in your log how closely you've adhered to the plan. If you came in under the 1,500-calorie limit, write a special word of congratulations to yourself. If you occasionally slip up—and don't we all?—write about that as well. Use these times as a way to review your plan and renew your commitment to your strategy and goal. A journal is a great way to use your mistakes to broaden your understanding of the particular goal at hand and your own strengths and weaknesses. Day after day, count your calories. Keep a record in your log. As a matter of course, look back for an overview of how you're progressing. The more days you stay under your limit, the more days you'll want to stay under your limit. After all, it would be a shame to break a record.

Weigh yourself once a week and record that weight in your log. If you remain faithful to your plan, you'll see that you'll lose at least one pound a week. This is very doable and is not detrimental to your health.

Getting in Shape

Getting in shape also lends itself very well to the goal-oriented log. The same technique applies. Begin with consulting your doctor and get approval for your goal and your plan. If you decide that you will walk your way to fitness, state your goals for how far you'd like to walk and with what frequency. Start your plan with walking for a short distance each day and slowly work your way up to the distance you'd like to reach.

The same idea works well with aerobics and weight lifting as well. You get the idea. Begin with your doctor and then write down how many jumping jacks and knee bends you want to do at each session. Start with small numbers and work your way up.

With weights, state your goal to bench press what you feel is realistic or how many pounds you'd like to leg lift.

No matter what goal you set for yourself, track your progress with your log. Nothing breeds success like success, and your journal will help you feature your successes.

Putting Pen to Paper

A perfect way to track your weight-lifting routine, the log lets you record each weight increase, each repetition increase, and each victory along the way.

The Greater Lesson

No matter how you put your log to work for you, you will have accomplished two very important things. First, you will have achieved particular goals that had importance to you. Congratulate yourself for a job well done and set a brand new goal or move on to a different type of journal.

Second, and this is just as important if not more so, you will have learned a technique that can help you achieve anything in life. You will know that, whether you want something on a personal or professional level, you can achieve it. It takes three simple steps:

1. State your goal.
2. Devise a plan.
3. Work the plan.

Remember, keeping a journal is not an end in itself, but a means to achieve other things. Look to your journal as a tool; the more you use it, the greater skill you'll develop. You can do this. You can achieve, because you have it within your power.

The Least You Need to Know

➤ Consider keeping a log if you want a daily record of your life.

➤ The log is a wonderful tool to use to help you achieve your goals.

➤ When you first get started writing in your log, practice by recording daily events and experiences.

➤ A three-step process can simplify the achievement of even the most complex goals.

➤ Once you've achieved your first goal, congratulate yourself and then move on to the next one.

Chapter 7

The Healing Journal

In This Chapter

➤ Recognizing that the power to heal often resides within you

➤ Harnessing the mind–body connection

➤ Writing about your doubts and fears is the first step to healing

➤ Discovering how physicians and psychiatrists have "prescribed" journaling for decades

➤ Using your healing journal to heal physical and emotional pain

Even with years of research and study behind them, scientists, psychiatrists, and physicians still don't fully understand the power of the human mind, the truth of the human heart, or the depth of the human soul. Yet we know the connection exists, and it has been the subject of extensive investigation and conjecture for generations. Researchers continue to formulate theories of why this connection works, yet no one can say for certain.

The power of the body, mind, and soul working together extends to all aspects of our being. If we believe we can do something, then we can do it, much as the engine in the children's book *The Little Engine That Could*. But that power isn't going to offer it-self to us out of the blue. We have to find it, cultivate it, and then use it. In this chapter, I'll show you how you can use your journal to help you channel your mind and spirit to help the healing process along.

You Gotta Have Faith

Whether or not you consider yourself a person of faith, the concept has come into our society as few others have. Many among us try to teach our children to believe they can do anything. We encourage patients to believe they will get well. We send soldiers into battle to accomplish the impossible. For thousands of years, we've understood that if you believe you can do something, you can.

Words of Wisdom

"What a piece of work is a man! How noble in reason, how infinite in faculty, in form and moving how express and admirable, in action how like an angel, in apprehension how like a god—the beauty of the world, the paragon of animals!"

—William Shakespeare, *Hamlet*

The Write Idea

The placebo effect occurs when patients improve or experience side effects to a placebo, usually a sugar pill, only because they believe they are taking real medication.

This chapter is about using your journal to help you heal yourself emotionally, physically, and spiritually. In order for it to work, however, you have to believe that your mind can affect your physical and mental well-being—the mind-body connection—and you have to have faith in your ability to do so. I'm not talking about faith in any religious sense, necessarily, but faith in yourself and in your ability to bring about change.

The Placebo Effect

When people living in the industrialized Western world fall ill, we go to a Western-trained physician who diagnoses our condition and prescribes appropriate treatment, usually in the form of medication.

Our Western philosophy of medicine, clinical and straightforward, works well most of the time, but even it takes into account the mind-body connection. Think of all the pains researchers take when they test a new medication.

They carefully design double-blind studies to keep test patients from knowing whether or not they're receiving the test medication. Researchers don't want patients to improve simply because they believe they will, a result called "the placebo effect." They want to assure themselves that the medication is the true source of improvement.

Although researchers take the mind-body connection and its attendant placebo effect very seriously, the actual practice of everyday medicine often gives it little thought. Overworked physicians tend to rely solely on tried and true therapies. However, in parts of world where Western medicine is nonexistent, the people must capitalize on what they do have—the power of the body and mind working together.

The Write Idea

In the past, and even still today in some parts of the world, people suffering from an illness would go to their local shaman for healing. Perhaps they complained of fever, a sore throat, or some sort of pain in the gut. The shaman would listen to the patient's description of the illness and "prescribe" the appropriate ritual. The patient often recovered either because the ailment would have gone away on its own in a few days anyway or because the patient believed in the shaman and his power. Very often, even though our Western doctors don't take the connection into account, the same healing process works for us as well.

What I've been leading up to with all this talk about the mind-body connection, faith, and the placebo effect is this: The power to heal can come from within; all you need to do is learn to tap into that power and believe in your ability to do so. You have a tremendous tool at your disposal, and keeping a healing journal will help you use it.

Finding the Power

Okay, by this time, you're probably beginning to think I'm a little wacky with all this talk about your internal healing powers. Good, because your first step in keeping a healing journal is to write about and work through your doubts.

Don't tell me about it. Get out your pen and tell your healing journal. Write about your doubts—we all have them—but also be open to the possibilities. Reread the section on the mind-body connection and the placebo effect if you want or read up on it in other books such as Bill Moyers's *Healing and the Mind.* Although it's perfectly normal to have doubts, you have to work through them and believe in your ability to affect change before it will happen.

The Write Idea

Bill Moyers, in his 1993 book *Healing and the Mind,* did a wonderful job of detailing the many theories about the connections between the human body and the human mind, and he did so in a way that even the layman can understand.

It's Just Like Chicken Soup!

For some people, writing about a traumatic event or medical problem to help a physical ailment sounds too weird. But if you take a moment to think about it, you'll see that it's not a whole lot different from lying in bed, eating chicken soup, and drinking hot tea when you've got a bad cold.

When your nose is stuffed and your head feels as big as a small continent, of course you want the cold to go away, but you also want to feel better. Chicken soup and hot tea are comfort foods. Their warmth reassures us, relaxes us, and makes us feel a little better. The cold remains with us, but because we feel more comfortable, we can cope better and perhaps even fall asleep for a while, allowing our body to do what it must to fight the cold.

This same principle works in much the same way for more serious and more painful conditions such as asthma and rheumatoid arthritis. Some newer studies have even dealt with people with hypertension and diabetes, and preliminary results show promise here as well. Writing about the distressful events of our life won't cure us, but in putting our thoughts on paper, we feel as though we have taken some control of a situation that we might otherwise perceive as uncontrollable, and we find this comforting. Comfort leads to a certain level of relaxation and easing of stress.

Freeing the body of stress aids the body in healing, in coping, and in compensating for certain conditions. Of course, the condition still exists, but with less stress, we're likely to feel better and enjoy a higher quality of life.

Write about your physical ills. Write about the emotional upsets and traumatic events in your life. Unburden yourself in the pages of your journal, give your stress an avenue of escape, and allow the power of body, mind, and soul to work together to heal you.

The Write Idea

Writing about your problems in a journal is very much like unburdening yourself to a best friend. The act of sharing makes you feel better emotionally as well as physically.

The Real Thing—Really!

Have I convinced you yet? Well, if you won't believe me, maybe you'll believe a trained physician and one of the most distinguished medical journals in the world.

An article in the April 14, 1999, issue of the *Journal of the American Medical Association* reports a study done by Joshua M. Smyth, Ph.D., of North Dakota State University in Fargo. His test patients consisted of 58 people with asthma and 49 patients with rheumatoid arthritis and asthma.

He took baseline assessments of their conditions such as symptoms, frequency and amount of medication, overall feelings, and how their condition affected their quality of life. Then he divided the patients into two groups. The first group, which he used as his control group, included 22 asthma patients and 19 with rheumatoid arthritis. The second group, the test group, consisted of the remaining patients, 39 asthma sufferers and 32 with rheumatoid arthritis.

He asked the patients in the first group, the control group, to keep a daily journal addressing neutral topics such as the weather, the sky, any subject that would fail to elicit a strong emotional response. Dr. Smyth also asked the test group to keep a journal, but he asked them to write about the most stressful events of their life. They could even write about their health problems and how they coped.

Both groups returned at two-week, two-month, and four-month intervals for follow-up evaluations of their condition. Those who wrote about their stressful experiences showed a marked reduction in symptoms and had "clinically relevant changes in health status at four months compared to those in the control group." In other words, their condition had improved. Some patients, under the supervision of their physician, were even able to reduce their daily medication.

Dr. Smyth is not alone in his research. A team of clinical psychologists and immunologists at Southern Methodist University and Ohio State University College of Medicine asked a group of test subjects to write about the traumatic experiences in their lives. During their follow-ups, they showed an increase in T-cell production, a drop in physician visits, fewer absentee days from work, and generally improved overall physical health.

When learning about such studies, the average person will shrug his shoulders and figure there might be something to it. The brilliant person, such as yourself, will look closely at the implications, recognize the powerful tool there for the taking, and use it to his advantage.

The Write Idea

The healing journal isn't intended to replace your physician; rather, it is a supplement to your physician, something that will allow you to focus on the mental while your doctor focuses on the physical aspects of your illness. As a matter of fact, you can also use your healing journal as a place to write down questions about your illness or your treatment that you may have for your doctor. On your next visit, you'll have them all right at hand. In fact, if you bring your journal with you, you can take notes on what the doctor tells you and have a permanent record.

Knowledge Is Power

As you gain knowledge about your condition, you'll probably feel more comfortable doing a little research on your own. Use your journal to record your findings and to comment on them. You may even learn about other choices available that you can discuss with your doctor. Little by little, you begin to take control of your own health care.

Because you have this knowledge, you can make informed decisions in partnership with your doctor that can lead to better and more effective treatment. With each piece of information you gain, your power grows and you gain control.

Recognize what part of yourself requires healing and write about it. Voice your concerns and your doubts to handle it. Once you get that out of the way, however, you need to press onward. Tell your friend, your journal, that no matter what looms ahead, you can deal with it.

The Write Idea

Education has always been the key to control and success. You have the ability to do the same and enhance your quality of life.

If you repeat the sentiment each time you write in your journal, you will eventually convince yourself on an emotional level, and that is what you want to reach. You want no uncertainty, no doubt, and no second-guessing in your mind or in your soul that you can take on the world and win.

The Aches and Pains of Life

Part of taking control is alleviating the pain and anxiety that come with physical ills. When you keep a healing journal, those are the things you should write about. Write about your discouragement as well as your hopes. For example, an entry in a healing journal might look like the following paragraph.

"The pain in my hip is really kicking up today, worse than in a long time. The doctor says it will take a few days before I feel the full effect of the new medication. I hope it'll bring me some relief. I can't remember the last time I've had a pain free day. Sometimes I get so frustrated with my arthritis that I just want to throw stuff against the wall and break it, but then I remind myself that it will do me no good."

The writer of this entry is bringing all her feelings out in the open and putting them on paper. Day after day of allowing oneself to vent while hoping to get better often leads to a better frame of mind, less pain, and better quality of life. No one knows why it works, but it does, and in the end, isn't that all that's necessary?

Emotional and Psychological Healing

In the 1950s, former student of Carl Jung and psychoanalyst Ira Progoff hit a rough time in his life. Separated from his wife and suffering from severe emotional strain, he began keeping a journal as a way to express himself and alleviate the stress. However, he found it did so much more for him.

It helped him put his problems in proper perspective, and in some cases, guided him toward solutions to his problems. In other instances, he found a way to deal with them. As a result, he reduced his stress level and experienced emotional healing.

He immediately recognized how the journal could help his patients, and so he began encouraging them to keep diaries. He wanted them to explore ideas, thoughts, and dreams within their journals, no matter how strange or off-the-wall they may have seemed. He wanted them to recount their emotions in certain situations and then give themselves feedback on those feelings.

Using the journal as a tool, his patients quickly found the power within themselves to heal psychologically. The journal gave them the means and the space to sort things out, to see things on paper. You, too, can profit from a journal to heal emotionally and psychologically.

Put It on Paper

Just as you would talk to your therapist about the things that bother you, "talk" to your journal. The advantage your journal has over your therapist is that your journal is always available to you. You don't have to depend on a specified time and place. And your journal will never look at its watch and tell you that your hour is over!

When something bothers you, write it down. When a question arises, record it. If you have a concern, voice it. For smaller emotional upsets, you and your journal, operating as a team, may very well be able to take you from hurt to healed. For clinical conditions such as depression, view your journal as an extension of your therapy. In either case, you are the one in control. You are the one who finds the power to rise above the pain and triumph.

The Birth of Pain

Emotional pain has its origins in all sorts of behavior, other people's as well as our own. Perhaps someone did you a wrong or you overreacted to a certain situation and said some things you shouldn't have. Now, every time you think of those events, you experience a hollow feeling in your chest, a pain that just doesn't seem to want to leave you.

These negative reactions not only prevent you from growing and healing spiritually, they actually drag you down and are detrimental to spiritual healing. Put yourself on the path to healing by going back to the source of the pain. Write about the incident with all the gory details. Unburden yourself into your journal.

Write about the importance of that event at the time it happened and then ask yourself about its importance to you a week later, a month later, a year later, maybe 10 years later, all the way up to the present moment.

You may surprise yourself when you find that, at this moment in time, the hurtful action really has very little significance to your life. Write about how the significance of the behavior has decreased over time. That being the case, isn't it safe to assume that, with more time, it will have even less impact? If this is true, why waste any more time and energy on it? Let go of it now and move on.

The Death of Pain

Pain will only die if we let it. Holding on to it and wearing it on our sleeve serves no purpose but to constantly remind us of it and to deepen the hurt. Like a festering wound, it does not heal. On the other hand, if you find it within yourself to take control, rise above the pain, and let go of it, you have taken the first steps toward healing.

Recognize the power you possess deep within you. Use your journal to find the power and tap into it. Utilize it as a companion to walk through the process with you. Like a best friend, it will allow you to rant and rave, express your doubts, and record new information. Take control of your life. Rise above the pain. Write your way to health.

The Least You Need to Know

➤ You have tremendous healing power at your disposal.

➤ The mind, body, and soul all work together in the healing process.

➤ You have to have faith in your ability to affect change for your healing journal to be effective.

➤ Your journal can help heal you physically, emotionally, and spiritually.

Chapter 8

The Cathartic Journal

In This Chapter

➤ Recognizing your emotional baggage and dealing with it

➤ Getting it off your chest and why that's good for you

➤ Exploring the various ways to keep your journal

➤ Reaping the benefits of catharsis

"I just had to get it off my chest!"

You know the feeling. Perhaps your emotions have been unsettled or a situation with someone has been building over a period of time. You feel as though you need to shout, yell, stomp your feet, let all your pent up frustrations loose. In the modern vernacular, you feel the need to "vent."

Don't punch holes in your walls and don't kick the cat. Instead, take a deep breath, relax for a moment, and write about it in your journal. To help you through the tough times, a cathartic journal can offer you a place to express your emotions freely without fear of judgment or recrimination.

Putting your feelings down on paper gives you the opportunity to think things through, calm down, and put everything in its proper perspective. When you can do that, you can begin to cleanse yourself of negative feelings and move on to a healthier, happier life. Don't ignore this very powerful tool that you have at your disposal.

Emotional Baggage

Life experiences leave us with a jumble of emotions both positive and negative. We find the positive feelings easy to deal with. Our spirits are buoyed when people treat us with love, joy, consideration, and thoughtfulness. Whenever we think about these experiences, the memories bring a smile and give us a positive outlook.

On the other hand, negative feelings engender an entirely different response. We might suffer hurt at someone's thoughtless words or anger at a rebuff. The sudden contempt of someone we had thought of as a friend wounds us deeply. Each of these encounters leaves its mark on our psyche, which we carry with us and often call our "emotional baggage."

The Write Idea

Because of the mind-body connection (discussed at length in Chapter 7, "The Healing Journal"), emotional upheaval, often referred to as stress, can actually cause physical conditions.

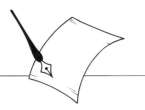

Putting Pen to Paper

If you have deep emotional pain that prevents you from functioning, don't depend solely on your journal to help you make everything right. You may benefit from professional therapy in conjunction with your journal.

For some of us, the baggage weighs much more heavily because it comes not from a single incident but from a series of events over a long period of time. Childhood trauma, sexual or physical abuse, mistreatment, cruelty, loss, and substance abuse come to mind as examples.

You would hope that over time the pain would lessen, but that only works if you don't allow yourself to think much about it. In many cases, however, time only allows us to contemplate it over and over again with no outlet and no one to talk to, which can make the pain run even deeper.

The Healing Process

Such wounds can leave lasting pain that may take a lifetime to overcome, but a journal can help. I remember one woman at one of my seminars who approached me after my presentation. She had suffered sexual abuse at the hands of her father as a child beginning at age two. The abuse continued until right around her twelfth birthday.

For years afterward, she went from psychologist to psychologist seeking relief from the demons that tormented her but met with little success. One relationship after another ended in failure, and when she had a son, she found that she didn't know how to be a loving mother to him. Then she found a doctor who asked her to keep a journal about her abuse. At first she didn't know what good it would do, but she did as he requested.

Soon she found that writing everything down helped her to see things more clearly. By putting it down on paper, she felt as though she no longer carried the entire burden. Little by little, with the aid of an understanding doctor and her journal, she healed, married, and mended her relationship with her son.

Thankfully, not all of us carry such emotional debris, but if journaling could do so much for a person with such deep wounds, think what it could do for you.

Holding On

We think about it and think about it and think about it some more. We fret and we fume, and the more we reflect on something that has happened to us, the more it bothers us. Some of us react by wanting to talk about it with anyone who will listen, but what we really want is for someone to confirm that we, and not the other person, are on the "right" side.

Often, the people around us get tired of listening to the same old story. As Don Quixote said in Miguel de Cervantes's masterpiece, *Don Quixote de la Mancha*, "'Tis the only comfort of the miserable to have partners in their woes." In other words, misery loves company, and after a while, we cannot find anyone who will offer the emotional support we need, and we find ourselves alone.

If you see yourself described here in any form, I suggest you continue reading this chapter for some ideas on keeping a cathartic journal. The simple techniques can help you forgive, forget, and move on.

Letting Go by Writing It Down

As discussed in previous chapters, Dr. Ira Progoff serendipitously discovered that keeping a journal through tough times can prove a tremendous emotional help. You need no such chance realization. You have his work to draw upon as well as hundreds, perhaps thousands, of therapists after him who have taken a page from his book and have guided their own patients to keep a journal.

The Write Idea

When we feel grief, keeping a journal to express our feelings of loss can help us sort through the anger, the fear, and the sorrow. Eventually, the process brings us to accept what we cannot change, and we give ourselves permission to heal and get on with life.

Words of Wisdom

In *A Grief Observed*, C. S. Lewis wrote, "Part of every misery is, so to speak, the misery's shadow or reflection: the fact that you don't merely suffer but have to keep on thinking about the fact that you suffer. I not only live each endless day in grief, but live each day thinking about living each day in grief." Such a state of mind makes for a wretched life, and you need not live like this.

Time and time again, therapists have demonstrated the value of the cathartic journal in helping patients to sort through their emotions and deal with them. You can benefit from what they have learned as you employ certain techniques and learn to put the pain behind you.

Being There

We all need someone to talk to freely, someone who will neither judge nor tell everyone he knows what we've told him.

Few of us are blessed with such confidants, and that's one of the reasons people go to therapists. They know that everything they tell a therapist will be held in the strictest confidence. In addition, the therapist will pass no judgment on their feelings or actions. Instead, the therapist will question the patient to guide him through the maze of his feelings.

Since it's impractical and expensive to make an appointment with a therapist for every emotional upset we encounter in life, it behooves us to take advantage of another very effective means we all have at our disposal, the journal. The first gift, then, is total availability. You always have a shoulder to cry on in total confidence.

The Write Idea

Many therapists continue to encourage their patients to keep a journal as part of their ongoing therapy. They have found that it helps their patients face their problems, deal with them, and move on in a more timely fashion.

The Joy of Freedom

The second gift your journal gives you is freedom from judgment. You can write anything you want within its pages, and it will never talk back to you or tell you that you did the wrong thing. What it will help you do is decide the rightness or wrongness of any action for yourself.

For this reason, you should write in your journal with the assurance that you can write in total honesty. Don't leave anything out. Delve into the deepest, darkest corners of your mind and, no matter what you find, put it on paper. You won't be able to deal with it effectively unless you can first bring it out into the light where you can see it and identify it.

Putting Pen to Paper

Once you work through your pain and get it all out of your system, you can move on to another type of journal to help you achieve something else in life.

Step by Step

As you open your book, begin with the understanding that you are going to keep this journal as a means of putting a hurtful incident behind you. Know that, when you set pen to paper or call up your computer program, you have that specific purpose in mind. Then begin to write.

During the first few days of keeping your journal, you should write down everything about the event that you can remember, right down to what color shirt you were wearing. Re-create the scene as best you can. Relate dialogue. Talk about the actions that the people involved took. Did someone slam a door? Did someone stomp out of the room? Did anyone cry?

Write about it until you can think of nothing more to include. Once completed, read the entire description at the end of your writing session and think about it until your next scheduled writing time.

Putting Pen to Paper

As you write about an upsetting event, you may find yourself reliving the experience all over again, complete with the emotional distress. Plow through it. You'll find that, in a very short time, you'll begin to feel better.

Let the River Flow

Before you begin to write again the next day, read your description of the event once more. Then close your eyes and permit yourself to feel the same raw emotions you felt at the time. Allow the anger, the pain, or the disappointment to flow unabated like a river flooded by a torrential rain. Name each emotion as it emerges and write about it.

Describe the hollowness in your chest, the need to cry, and the desire to stomp your feet as though you were a child throwing a temper tantrum. If you cried, write about how that made you feel. If you felt disappointment, write about that, too, and why. You must have had expectations that didn't materialize; what were they? Write them down.

Although reliving a painful event may cause renewed suffering, we should look at the process almost as if we're taking that aching package we've been carrying around with us and handing it off to someone else. With that done, we find it at least a little easier to bear and much easier to move on to more positive things.

This part of the process might go on for several days, depending on the complexity of the emotions and how long you have kept them bottled up inside. Some diarists find this to be the most difficult part of the process because the writer experiences those raw emotions all over again.

Feelings, Nothing More Than Feelings

As you keep your journal, remember that, like a therapist, it cannot and will not judge you, and truthfully, you can neither defend nor condemn your feelings. Feelings and preferences are what they are, born of creation and experience.

Words of Wisdom

"We judge ourselves by what we feel capable of doing, while others judge us by what we have already done."

—Henry Wadsworth Longfellow

It's important that you don't pass judgment on the feelings you express in your journal, as this will only inhibit you from expressing them honestly.

A Jury of One

Although you can't judge your feelings, you can certainly judge your actions because, whether you admit it to others or not, you know if you acted in an ethical way. Statistically, only a small percentage of the population has no true idea of right or wrong due to mental capacity, brain dysfunction, or how they were raised. The odds are, you fall into the category of people who know the difference.

True, no one but you knows what was in your heart; however, others do perceive your actions and then judge for themselves the kind of person you are.

Onward and Upward

Once you've written about your pain and its source, you're halfway there. The next step is to take each identified emotion and action and write about them. A simple method is to begin with a list of incomplete sentences that you need to finish, a kind of "fill in the blanks" sort of exercise.

Once you get the idea, you can probably list hundreds, but let me suggest a few to get you started. Feel free to finish these sentence in the book or in your journal:

➤ Right now I feel ...

_____

_____

_____

➤ It made me so angry I wanted to ...

_____

_____

_____

➤ I'm so sad I wish I could ...

_____

_____

_____

➤ I hurt so much I want to ...

_____

_____

_____

➤ I miss him or her and wish I could ...

_____

_____

_____

➤ If I had to do it over again, I would ...

_____

_____

_____

➤ I don't understand how he or she could ...

_____

_____

_____

➤ Did I do anything to provoke ...?

_____

_____

_____

➤ I could have defused the situation by ...

_____

_____

_____

➤ I feel afraid because ...

_____

_____

_____

➤ I feel frustrated because ...

_____

_____

_____

69

➤ If I could change things, I would …

_____

_____

_____

You know better than anyone which of these sentences apply to you or if none of them apply. Use them as a basis for your own contemplation and exploration.

Don't be afraid to let your imagination go wild. This is, after all, an emotional exercise in speculative history, a way to learn for future experiences. Describe the way you wish the event had happened or how you wish you had reacted. This process gives you a way to unburden yourself of ambivalent feelings and prepare yourself for future experiences.

How Long Can This Go On?

How long it takes depends on you and how deep your hurt runs. The more profound the emotional trauma, the longer it may take. But don't feel as though you're on any time schedule. Take as long as you need.

If, for some reason, this technique doesn't work for you immediately, have a little patience. It may take weeks or months. Emotional injury often leaves deeper scars than any physical wound, and the longer you've been harboring the hurt, the longer it will take for you to come to terms with it and get it all out of your system.

Other Techniques

Once you have taken yourself through the steps I've just described, you may think of some methods you might like to try. I encourage you to go ahead and make the effort. See if they work for you and, if they do, continue using them. Also allow yourself the luxury of formulating and attempting others. You may pleasantly surprise yourself and find something of tremendous help to you.

On the other hand, there are some other methods I'd like to tell you about. You might give them a try as well. Pick and choose the ones that give you the biggest measure of freedom to tap into your feelings and let them flow unabated.

The Broken Record

Write about the incident for several days, even weeks, until you can't stand it anymore. At some point, you'll very happily let go of it and move on to something else. Just think about times when the news covers a particular subject day after day after weary day. After three, five, or ten days, you just don't want to hear about it anymore.

The same will hold true for you. The monotony of the subject will bore you to tears, and besides, you will have said everything you can possibly say on the subject. Free of it, you'll look forward to writing about something else the next day and perhaps even moving on to a different style of journal.

Automatic Writing

Sigmund Freud, the father of modern psychology, took the study of the human psyche from the shadows of superstition to the bright light of day. He began to study the workings of the mind, the meaning of dreams, and how early experiences affected people through their whole life. One of his theories claimed that sometimes we blurt things out because they're what we truly think. We let them slip, hence the term "Freudian slip."

With automatic writing, also sometimes called "stream-of-conscious writing," you allow yourself one Freudian slip after another. Let your fingers fly across the page, writing or typing anything that comes to mind. Don't edit what you write or censure yourself in any way. At first you'll write what is uppermost in your mind, but you'll eventually peel away the layers to get down to your deepest emotions.

When you put them on paper, it's as though you hand them off to somebody else to handle, and you can rid yourself of them once and for all.

The Write Idea

Not everything you write will have deep meaning. Especially when you begin to use this technique, you'll notice that some of your writing will be frivolous, fantastic, or downright ridiculous. Don't read too much into it. Even Freud said, "Sometimes a cigar is just a cigar."

Way to Go

As with most things in life, the cathartic journal offers you several paths to follow. Pick the one that best meets your needs. Remember that you need to face the pain, identify its source, and deal with it. Having done that, you can finally move on to a happier and healthier life.

The Least You Need to Know

➤ We all carry emotional baggage with us.

➤ Venting is a healthy way to deal with emotions.

➤ Your cathartic journal not only helps you vent, it gives you the opportunity to put things in perspective.

➤ With a little imagination, you can write about things the way you wish they had happened to prepare you for future experiences.

Chapter 9

The Unsent Letter

"Have I told you that I love you?"

What a wonderful thing to hear from that special someone in your life, but sadly, too many of us feel uncomfortable talking about our feelings. Have you told the people in your life that you care about them? Sometimes we never fully realize how we feel about people until after they are no longer part of our lives. Perhaps they've moved a great distance away or have died, leaving nothing but memories behind.

Despite their absence, we sometimes still have the need to tell them what is on our mind and in our heart. The unsent letter journal may offer you the means to get these feelings off your chest. It allows you to say exactly what is on your mind without the fear of rejection, ridicule, or judgment.

Kissin' Cousins

The unsent letter, a close relative of the cathartic journal, which was covered in the preceding chapter, differs from its cousin in two ways. First, although, as in the cathartic journal, you write about something that bothers you, you write it as a letter to a specific person. Second, in this journal, you elaborate on something you truly wanted to say but never did.

Furthermore, whereas the purpose of the cathartic journal is to purge negative emotions, the unsent letter can be used to express positive as well as negative emotions. True, you can write about how much someone may have hurt you or angered you, but you can also tell the person how much you miss or care about him or her.

Sharing Secrets

As the writer of an unsent letter, you should think of your journal as the person you would like to talk to or share something with. Now is the time to tell the person exactly how you feel or how he or she hurt you. You can express feelings of love, gratitude, or respect. You can also say that you feel he or she's overbearing and manipulative. In short, you can express exactly what you have in your heart and on your mind.

If at any time you feel you need to express feelings to a specific person, the unsent letter is an excellent vehicle. You'll feel better while maintaining your emotional privacy.

Putting Pen to Paper

You can begin writing this journal as if you were writing a letter, complete with any salutation you would ordinarily use such as, "Dear John."

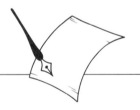

Putting Pen to Paper

The person you write to can be alive and live nearby—maybe even in the same house!—or can live halfway around the world or have passed out of this life.

From the Sublime to the Reserved

Some people wear their heart on their sleeve, letting the whole world know their deepest emotions. With no compunction about sharing their feelings, they are quick to smile, hug, or cry. To describe them, we use words like "emotional" and "affectionate."

At the other end of the spectrum are people we often describe as reserved. Their reticence to share their innermost thoughts and feelings might be a defense mechanism to protect them from emotional hurt, or it might be just a result of the way they were raised. Sometimes they take that protection to the extreme, and they appear cold and unfeeling.

They prefer not to make their feelings an open book. They don't tell people close to them that they love them. They very rarely initiate a hug or offer a word of encouragement. That doesn't mean they have no feelings. It only means they either don't see the necessity of expressing themselves or fear rejection.

A Secret Crush

Remember your first crush? You probably kept it a well-guarded secret, at least for a time, for fear of what your friends would say and, of course, because you didn't want to be rejected. And who could blame you? What if that person didn't feel the same way about you? Good grief! You would have died of embarrassment.

Most of us overcome those fears and, as we mature, find ourselves better able to tell that special someone that we love him or her. Some of us, though, never find the words or the courage. We fall in love but can't bring ourselves to reveal how we feel.

And then the unmentionable happens. The person disappears from our life. People often slowly disappear from our life because we fail to keep in touch, or we may lose them more dramatically through death. In either case, too many feelings remain bottled up inside. Too many things left unsaid or undone will, over time, weigh us down emotionally.

The Write Idea

Grief counselors often encourage people in mourning to write unsent letters to someone close who has died. The technique allows the writer to open the floodgates of emotion that have been bottled up and allow the feelings to flow without reserve.

Let It All Out

If you count yourself among these more reserved souls, you may find many benefits in keeping an unsent letter journal. Just as the women of the Japanese royal court felt sufficiently free to write about their deepest feelings in their pillow books, you, too, should take confidence in that freedom when you write in your journal without fear of rejection or as a dress rehearsal for the real thing.

To Whom It May Concern

We humans are social creatures. We join clubs and organizations so we can associate with others who share common beliefs and philosophies. We nurture relationships of all kinds, from casual acquaintances to deep, intimate bonds. For most of these relationships, a light, easy-going type of association fills the bill.

The Write Idea

Our willingness to express our emotions openly is largely the result of our upbringing and culture. If we grow up in an environment in which people regularly articulate a wide range of emotions, then odds are we will, too. If, on the other hand, you grew up in an environment with people unwilling to express their emotions, you, too, are most likely reserved.

We might enjoy talking about politics, clothes, cooking, or cars with others who share our enthusiasm for a particular subject. None of this requires much in the way of emotional expression.

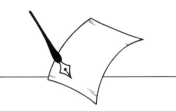

Putting Pen to Paper

Freeing yourself from deep emotional pain may help you come out of your reserved shell. Using a cathartic journal to deal with a bad experience can help you move on to an unsent letter. Once you've put your feelings about someone on paper, you may find it easier to express yourself openly.

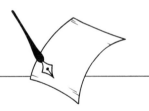

Putting Pen to Paper

For some people, the act of putting the feelings into words and writing them down serves as a kind of rehearsal. With a few rehearsals under their belt, they find the courage to approach that special person face to face and tell him or her exactly how they feel.

But when it comes to people whom we care about deeply, emotional expression plays a major role. These are the people who matter most to us, yet we very often lack the courage to tell them that we love them, that we forgive them, or that we miss them. We either see it as a sign of weakness or fear their rejection. Address these people in your journal, one at a time, and unleash your bottled up emotions.

The Unsent Love Letter

Have you ever wished you had told someone you loved him or her while the person was still a part of your life? I think we all have at one time or another. I have met many people who tell me they wish they had told a loved one of their feelings before the person died, for example.

I remember a young woman in one of my journaling workshops who said she wished she had told her father that she loved him before he died. When I asked her why she hadn't, she replied, "I know my father loved me, but he never said so while we were growing up. It just wasn't something you said in our house. Just before he died, I wanted to hear him say it, but he never did, but I still need to tell him how I feel."

She also told me that she dreamed often of her father wandering aimlessly, joylessly along a beach. She interpreted her dreams as her father wanting to hear of her love as much as she had wished for it while he was still alive. With tears in her eyes, she told me, "Now it's too late."

It's never too late. Take your book in your hand and start to write. In this young woman's case, I told her to start writing a letter to her father telling him how much she loved him and why. I suggested that she write about all the wonderful times—vacations, games, secrets—they shared while she was growing up and her father was still living. I encouraged her to take the opportunity in her journal to tell her father exactly how he made her feel and how much she loved him when he was living and still loves him now.

You're probably not going to get everything off your chest in one sitting. It may take weeks of writing to someone, telling him or her everything you feel. That's all right. Take all the time you need. Express yourself as you have never done before. You'll know when you're finished. You'll experience a feeling of completeness, as though you had a job to do. And now that you've done it and done it well, you can rest happy.

By the way, I heard from that young woman several weeks later. She had kept her journal during that time and poured out her soul. Now unburdened, she dropped me a note of thanks. She also told me she still dreamed of her father, but now he walked along the beach with a smile on his face.

You, too, can find the peace you seek by writing of your love for a parent, a child, a spouse, or someone else who has held a special place in your heart. Open the pressure valve and let your feelings out. Unburden yourself and feel complete.

The Unsent Letter of Forgiveness

I forgive you.

These three little words are tremendously powerful. We all have disagreements from time to time. We say things or make choices that can hurt others or are on the receiving end of such actions. The hurt may run so deep that, at the time, we just can't bring ourselves to offer forgiveness no matter how much we realize on an intellectual level that it was a mistake.

As time passes, we may put things in perspective and realize that it wasn't so important after all, and we become willing to forgive. However, the person we wish to forgive is gone. We'll never see the person again, and this need to forgive weighs heavily on our mind.

Your unsent letter journal can allow you to pour out all the things you feel, what should have been done and said, how it could have been prevented,

Words of Wisdom

"Love gives naught but itself and takes naught but from itself. Love possesses not nor would it be possessed; For love is sufficient unto love."

–Kahlil Gibran, *The Prophet*

Putting Pen to Paper

So many of us know people who are reticent to express their love for us, and we'd love to hear them tell us, just once, that they care. Maybe taking the initiative by telling them how we feel about them will give them the courage to say what is in their heart.

and all the other things whirling around in your mind. Your journal provides the outlet you need to put things in perspective and get past it.

Consider using your journal to write to the person about the injury. Once you've sorted it all out on paper, have a talk with the person to see how you can repair the damage done to your relationship.

Setting Things Straight in a Letter

Ever wish you could go back in time and set things straight or correct someone's misconception? You're certainly not alone! Since that darn time machine hasn't been invented yet, why not use the unsent letter to go back in time? Whether or not anyone will ever see what you write doesn't matter. All that matters is that you set the record straight about what happened.

Words of Wisdom

"We pardon to the extent that we love."

—François, Duc de La Rochefoucauld, *Sentences et maximes morales*

The Angry Unsent Letter

Have you ever been teased? Ill-treated? Snubbed? Most of us have, and the experience has left us feeling powerless and angry. We want to strike back at the person who has caused the pain, but we can't because he or she is bigger or more powerful, so we let the anger build. Don't let this happen to you. Take the healthier path.

Words of Wisdom

"I should have no objection to go over the same life from its beginning to the end: requesting only the advantage authors have, of correcting in a second edition the faults of the first."

—Benjamin Franklin, *Autobiography*

The Write Idea

Sometimes it really is better to leave some things unsaid. If telling the truth to someone will needlessly cause him or her pain, but you feel the need to get the facts off your chest, you might consider setting the record straight in an unsent letter instead.

Write the person a letter. Without fear, talk about how hurt and disappointed you are with him or her. Write about your anger and how you'd really like to respond to the person's action.

The process might take days or weeks depending on the extent of your anger, but eventually, you'll get it all out.

Facing Fear and Anxiety with a Letter

We all experience fear from time to time. Fear of physical or emotional pain, fear of legal action, fear of what others will think of us—all sorts of fears figure into the mix of our daily lives. While we tend to think of fear and anxiety as negative emotions, they serve a purpose, and when working correctly, they spur us to some action to ensure our survival.

Almost anything can make us anxious or afraid—driving on busy highways, the thought of death or illness, taking a big test, a meeting with the boss. Why not write a letter to the source of the fear or anxiety—it may not be another person—in your journal? Let your letter serve as a sounding board and as a means of sorting things out. You'll be surprised at how putting your worries down on paper and addressing the source of your concerns directly can make you feel better.

Words of Wisdom

"What I've learned about being angry with people is that it generally hurts you more than it hurts them."

—Oprah Winfrey

Words of Wisdom

"He has not learned the lesson of life who does not every day surmount a fear."

—Ralph Waldo Emerson, *Society and Solitude*

79

Words of Wisdom

"I feel as if I were a piece in a game of chess, when my opponent says of it: That piece cannot be moved."

—Søren Kierkegaard, *Either/Or*

Frustrated? Write a Letter

We've all felt like that chess piece at one time or another. It happens when people and events move around you and you have no power to change anything. It happens when you argue with a bill collector who doesn't believe you when you tell him that you sent the check in months ago. It happens when your mother-in-law won't keep her nose out of your business. It happens when your insurance company won't pay for your medical bills. I can almost see you nodding your head. You know exactly what I mean. Sometimes the frustration lasts for hours, sometimes weeks, sometimes longer. And what do you do while your irritation grows? How can you keep your wits about you while you try to solve the problem? Write. You'll be getting your negative emotions off your chest and, just maybe, creating a solution to your dilemma.

Putting Pen to Paper

If you know someone who is terminally ill, you might encourage him to keep a journal in the style of the unsent letter. Perhaps the person has things on his mind that he'd like to tell someone, to set things straight or to express love. Particularly if he's been emotionally reserved all his life, he might jump at the chance to write things that, until now, have been left unsaid. If he is too ill to write, offer to record his letters for him or to transcribe what he says into a tape recorder. You'll not only be helping the person leave this life with a bit more peace of mind, you'll be helping to create a legacy for loved ones left behind.

All Your Secrets

We all travel through life with secrets of the heart—some good, some dark. The unsent letter journal offers you a means of expressing yourself to the people you wish to communicate with on an emotional level without fear. It gives you the freedom to write from the depths of your heart and soul without the embarrassment you might otherwise feel in a face-to-face meeting. Yet, because you articulate your emotions within the pages of a book, you give the special people in your life a way to know how you feel.

Anyone, even the most emotionally demonstrative person, can benefit from the unsent letter at various times in his or her life. If you have the intention of talking to that particular person anyway, it allows you to put it on paper first, hash it out, and get the words just right before you actually talk to the person.

If you have no intention of actually telling the person during your lifetime, then you always have the option of leaving it behind as a gift for the people who held a place in your heart.

The Least You Need to Know

➤ Write your unsent letter just as you would if you were planning to send it off.

➤ The unsent letter is ideal for expressing deep emotions—both positive and negative.

➤ You can use your journal as a sounding board to get your thoughts together before facing an uncomfortable situation.

➤ The unsent letter can be a priceless legacy for loved ones.

The Theme Journal

Parades and high school dances have themes. Town celebrations have themes. Why not journals? At certain times, situations arise that capture or require our attention for weeks, months, and even years: planning a wedding, the expected birth of a baby, the college experience, the illness and impending death of a loved one. All come with the territory known as life, and each presents us with opportunities to learn, grow, and cope.

At such times, we find ourselves in a whirl of activity and experience the full gamut of emotions. Your journal, very specific to this particular time in your life, can act as an outlet for all your frustrations and as a place for you to celebrate the victories, both big and small.

Whatever has your attention at this time in your life, you can utilize the theme journal to get through the events in the most productive and least stressful way.

The Theme

Whether you realize it or not, you live a pretty sensational life worthy of recording in a journal. During the times when certain events take over your life and surrender seems the easier course, you should switch gears to keep a theme journal.

You won't have to spend time looking for a particular theme. It will find you. When you decide it's time to move, for example, the planning, the forms, and the logistics of the whole process seem to loom larger than anything else in your life. Because it takes so much of your time and attention, I'd say that this would be a natural application for a theme journal if I ever saw one.

A wedding is another perfect occasion for a theme journal. Any bride-to-be, and her mother, will tell you that the months leading up to that special day are filled with tension and activity. Your head whirls with concerns about flowers, music, photographers, tuxedos, gifts, invitations, caterers, rings, attendants, and—take a deep breath here—the all-important wedding dress. The list never seems to end, and sometimes you feel as though you're going to explode.

If you've changed jobs, done taxes, renovated a house, gone through a divorce, navigated through a lawsuit, or worked for a political candidate, you have intimate knowledge of the full gamut of emotions that such activities can bring into your life. Sometimes you can pat yourself on the back and smile with satisfaction that something went according to plan. But at other times, when nothing seems to go right, you'd love to just scream. Go ahead and scream for about three seconds, then sit down and tell your troubles to your journal.

Life Happens

Whatever circumstances you find thrust upon you, accept them as part of life. Nobody ever promised a stress-free existence. If you must deal with a sad situation, your theme journal can help you face it and cope with the least amount of trauma. For a happier situation, like planning a wedding, your journal can serve as a way to keep track of plans and people and, in the process, can lower your stress.

Words of Wisdom

"I never travel without my diary. One should always have something sensational to read in the train."

—Oscar Wilde, *The Importance of Being Earnest*

Putting Pen to Paper

As soon as you know of your involvement in a foreseeable event, begin keeping a theme journal. Not only will it help you get control of things from the beginning, it will help you learn better planning techniques for future events and will maintain a contemporary record of things as they progress.

In either case, you have to learn to say, "All right, this is the way things are." Once you fully understand the meaning of that little sentence, you can move on to try to deal with all the things you must. If you can change something for the better, then by all means pursue that path. If you can see no way to change an unpleasant outcome, then accept things as they are and learn to cope the best you can.

Hold the Sauce!

Throughout the scenario playing itself out in your life, you're going to have to make a variety of decisions. Should you serve tartar sauce or cocktail sauce with the shrimp cocktail at the reception? You like cocktail sauce. Your groom likes tarter sauce. Then, to complicate matters, your maid of honor suggests lemon only. All the while, the caterer waits patiently for a word from you.

As Abraham Lincoln said, "You can't please all of the people all of the time." Take what he said to heart as well as everyone's suggestions and record them in your journal. Consider the reality of the situation and then make the best decision you can. For example, you and your groom most likely will not get the opportunity to eat much at your reception, so does it really matter what you and your groom prefer? Have the discussion with yourself in your journal. You may conclude that, since the caterer has more experience with people's preferences, you should defer to his expertise.

The Write Idea

Keeping an effective journal of any kind can help lower your stress level because you feel as though you have some control over the situation. In turn, this boosts your immune system and helps you feel better physically. Feeling better gives you more energy to deal with any problems that may arise. This, in turn, lowers stress, and the positive cycle continues.

Wade Through the Maze

Of course, this is an oversimplification, but you get the idea. Discuss it. Sort through the garbage and get down to reality in your journal—then make your decision. Of course you're going to have doubts, but don't let them haunt you. Everyone has doubts about their decisions, but if you really believe you've chosen the right path, stick with it.

I can't imagine taking on any big project without experiencing doubts, indecision, irritation, disappointment, pleasure, and yes, even satisfaction. If you're in the process of renovating a house, you'll wonder if the darker paneling in the den will make the room look too small. Should you install a pedestal sink instead of a vanity in that little bathroom?

The Write Idea

If you use a theme journal during a project for which you have to hire contractors, it's an excellent place to record names, addresses, phone numbers, and other pertinent contact information.

Then, of course, you have to deal with all the little problems that arise along the way. How do you react when the contractor calls and says he can't make it to your house today? What do you say when the carpet store calls to tell you that the carpet you absolutely love has been discontinued?

Get Out of the Rut

Your frustration level will probably reach an all-time high while you try to keep your temper and anxiety under control, not an easy task unless you have an outlet. You might turn to someone close to you who will allow you to vent. At times like this, we often end up talking incessantly about our problems, concerns, and plans. While friends and loved ones are certainly there to listen to you and support you, you certainly don't want to become a drag.

Don't rehash the same stories over and over. You don't want to bore your friends, and you need to look for a new perspective on the whole state of affairs for yourself. So, once you've expressed yourself, thank these wonderful people for their time and then move on to another outlet: your journal.

Write incessantly if you need to about all the frustrations, concerns, joys, and funny moments. Describe how it all makes you feel. Share your plans and what you'd like to achieve through this episode. Whether a happy or sorrow-filled situation, it nonetheless takes its toll through stress. Use your journal to help you cope.

Feeling the Pressure

If you feel a lot of pressure, you're probably not operating at your best. Instead of dealing with the things you must, you might find yourself preoccupied with emotional issues. Granted, you have to get it out of your system, but don't use your time talking about it. Write about it.

People, though gracious enough to listen, often offer no constructive advice for a variety of reasons. Perhaps they've never had the same experience or lack the ability to see your point of view. Maybe they have no practical knowledge of the project or people involved. And then maybe, just maybe, they have made it a policy never to give advice.

On the other hand, I'm sure you know a plethora of people who would willingly give you all the advice in the world on any subject you could mention without knowing all the little details of your circumstances. For the most part, their council—though well-intentioned—gives you little guidance.

Inner Guidance

Learn to trust yourself. Intimately acquainted with the situation, including the people, you have all the information you need to know what to do and how to react. You only need a sounding board. Your journal can serve that purpose for you.

Write in your journal as though it's a close friend, able to give you all the time in the world, and listen with infinite patience. Write about what is going on in your life at this particular juncture. Tell how this big project influences your relationships and how you spend your time.

If you can't wait until you can bring the matter at hand to a conclusion, don't be afraid to voice that sentiment in your journal. Speculate as to how you can speed up the process. If you will miss your involvement in this project when it ends, write about that, too. Try to think of another project that might bring you as much satisfaction. If your frustration is running high, put the feeling into words and get it out of your system. Is there anything you can do to alleviate that aggravation? Use your imagination. Get creative and try to come up with a way to make things easier on yourself.

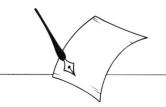

Write about it all within the pages of your journal and even ask it for advice. Don't expect your book to talk back to you, but by asking questions, you plant the question in your subconscious, and believe it or not, the counsel you seek will eventually come to you.

Imagine different scenarios and ways in which everything could conclude. Work out all the possibilities you can think of in your journal. Choose the best of all possible outcomes and use it as a guide to get you where you want to go.

Putting Pen to Paper

Sometimes the theme journal overlaps with the cathartic journal. That's fine. Pick and choose, mix and match the ideas of several different types of journals to create a hybrid that meets your particular needs.

Sleep On It

Believe it or not, the expression "sleep on it" has a measure of truth to it. When you have something on your mind, whether you're wondering how to handle a tricky situation or trying to answer a puzzling question, your subconscious continues to work on it while you occupy yourself with other concerns. I know you've experienced it. We all have.

You may have spent hours trying to figure out your problem, but had no success. The pieces of the puzzle don't seem to fit together, and you feel as though you have to walk away from it for a time to do something else. Then suddenly, the solution to the problem hits you like a bolt out of the blue, and you wonder why you hadn't thought of it before.

You didn't think of it before because your brain had not yet put all the pieces together to make sense of the information. While you were cooking, preparing your presentation for work, or negotiating traffic, a portion of your brain continued to work on the problem without you even knowing it. When your mind finally came up with an acceptable answer, it let you know with a jolt of recognition.

Keeping a theme journal and knowing that you can take advantage of the ability of your subconscious mind to work independently can help you deal more comfortably with tough decisions and setbacks inherent in any big project. When you understand that concept, your stress level goes down drastically because you know you will eventually find the answer.

The Write Idea

The conscious mind and the subconscious mind can, and often do, work independent of each other. Much like an operating system on a computer, the brain handles multiple functions at one time. So, while you're driving down the freeway, your mind is working on your problem in the background.

The Three-Step Method

With most things, no matter how big they seem at first, if you break them down into smaller and simpler steps, they suddenly become easier to deal with. Let me suggest a three-step method for writing in your theme journal: overview, update, and control.

The First Step

Start at the beginning and write an overview of the current situation. Include its beginnings, its developments, and how you arrived at this point. Take care to write about all the people involved and all the twists and turns. If it's terribly complicated, take two or three days to describe it. You don't have to do it all in one sitting. Take as much time as you need, but do your best to make it as clear as possible.

During this part of the process, take time to write about your feelings. Don't be afraid to admit that you'd rather not be involved or that you'd choose to do things differently. These are honest feelings. Once you recognize your feelings on the subject, you can consider the possibility of doing something about them.

Let me share a few suggested points of departure for you to consider when writing about your feelings in a theme journal:

➤ I can't wait until this is all over because …

➤ I'm looking forward to working on this project because …

➤ I dread working on this project because …

➤ I wish I had never started this because …

➤ I'm the best person to do this because …

➤ I believe someone else would be better at this because …

➤ This project is my responsibility because …

➤ I love working on this because …

➤ Working on this project will help me learn to …

➤ I see this project as an opportunity to …

I know you can think of many others, but these are some suggestions to get you started. Once you begin, you'll think of many other phrases that will lead you in some very interesting directions.

The People

You should write about the people involved as though you were sketching characters in a novel. Describe each person's physical characteristics as well as their inner character. Consider these questions when you write about them.

➤ Do you trust them?

➤ Do you feel you can work with them?

➤ Will they be of help to you or a hindrance?

➤ If you are the helper, what can you contribute?

➤ Do you feel comfortable working with them?

➤ Are they willing to teach you what they know?

➤ Are they willing to learn from you?

➤ Do they share information willingly?

➤ Are they hard workers?

➤ Do they smile easily?

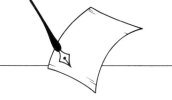

Putting Pen to Paper

We can't ever read people's minds to know their true nature, but their behavior reflects their thoughts and character. Be more observant of the people around you. What you see in their behavior will teach you much about what is in their mind.

The questions may appear simple, but you should give them some thought before answering. The answers will give you some insight into the kind of person you might be working with.

Once you have the situation down on paper, as well as your feelings and the people involved, you've taken the very first step in this journey that will last as long as you need it to.

Step Two

With the overview out of the way, update the state of affairs on a daily basis. As new people appear on the scene, introduce them. Write about them and give any future readers a sense of their place in this particular set of circumstances.

Putting Pen to Paper

Write as clearly and concisely as you can. Although you're writing this journal to help you through specific times, you'd probably like to have it as a complete record for yourself in the coming years as well as a chronicle to help future readers understand the situation.

As the "plot" takes its twists and turns, explain how they came about and if they will prove advantageous or detrimental to your situation. Don't be afraid to bring your imagination into play and try to predict how things will work out. Day by day, update your journal with all the particulars so that anyone reading it will understand everyone and everything clearly.

As you go through this process, you'll feel as though your emotions are as level as a roller coaster. Expect ups and downs. The best thing you can do, however, is accept them and write about them in all their stark honesty.

Step Three

As you update your diary on the progression of the project at hand and how you feel, take the third step: Take control. To do this, accept what is happening, accept your feelings, then resolve to take action.

For example, if one of your well-intentioned aunts has decided you need her help in planning your wedding, it could give you a feeling of frustration. You love her, but at the same time, recognize that you have very little in common when it comes to choosing food, flowers, or anything else for that matter!

At the same time, you don't want to hurt good ol' auntie's feelings. Discuss the dilemma in your journal. Consider possible ways of talking with her to gently refuse her kind offer. In fact, you may even think of something she can do quite well for you, such as coming up with lists of caterers, photographers, and printers. She'll feel useful, you haven't hurt her feelings, and she will produce something you can use.

Don't let the situation debilitate you. Don't let your feelings overwhelm you. Take control. Recognize the power you have within and move on to succeed.

The Times of Your Life

Life happens. We cry, we laugh, we cope with change. As overwhelming as some things may seem, they only take over our lives if we let them. You have the intelligence, the means, and the ability to find solutions, deal with setbacks, and move forward in triumph. Keeping a theme journal will not only help you survive what could be a trying time in your life, but help you learn from it and take control of it with style and grace.

The Least You Need to Know

➤ Situations need not take over your life.

➤ Learn to trust yourself and your ability to make decisions.

➤ The theme journal allows you not only to vent but to keep a contemporary record of the situation or project as it unfolds.

➤ The three-step method helps you take control.

Chapter 11

The Reflective Journal

In This Chapter

➤ Your journal as a reflection of you

➤ Understanding what makes you tick

➤ Analyzing your character

➤ Making positive changes

For character development, the reflective journal serves like none other. A basic understanding of the human psyche, your own psyche in particular, will help you navigate through the maze of the mind to gain a better understanding of your priorities, motivations, and actions.

With that knowledge, you can determine your best character traits as well as your weaknesses. You can learn to nurture your positive characteristics to expand them and keep them strong, while working on your weaknesses to correct them.

This exercise in character development is never an easy one, but it is by far one of the most interesting you could undertake. In the course of learning about yourself, you will necessarily learn about people in general, a most valuable bit of knowledge to have.

Where's My Mirror?

"Let's talk a little about the reflective journal," I suggested at a workshop one day.

One man with a particularly wry sense of humor exclaimed, "I'm sorry, I can't do that … I forgot my mirror."

Words of Wisdom

"The literature of the inner life is very largely a record of struggle with the inordinate passions of the social self."

—Charles Horton Cooley, *Human Nature and the Social Order*

Of course, everyone chuckled, and I went on with the presentation, but I also made it clear that the gentleman wasn't too far off the mark. A reflective journal is one that reflects our character through our writing. In effect, it becomes the mirror to your heart, mind, and soul.

As you become adept in its use, you will draw from deep within you things you may never have realized about yourself. You will learn what makes you tick, what moves you emotionally, and what spurs you to action.

Before telling you how to keep a reflective journal, a basic understanding of your psyche is in order. This information will make it easier for you and will make your journaling far more effective.

Psyched!

Let's take a brief lesson in psychology so you better understand what you're looking for. According to Sigmund Freud, the father of modern psychology, the human psyche consists of three parts, the id, the superego, and the ego. Each of the parts plays a different role in our emotions, thoughts, and actions. One of the very popular TV shows from the 1960s, *Star Trek*, very aptly demonstrates these three elements in the three main characters.

Dr. McCoy was the highly emotional, impulsive character. He represented the id, always ready to spring into action without considering the consequences. Mr. Spock, on the other hand, filtered all his choices through his very strict moral code and acted accordingly. He represented the superego. Captain Kirk represented the ego, the one in command who decided what action to take.

If you put them all together, you have a complete and complex human being very much like yourself. Now you must discover which part of your psyche is the strongest, and which needs the most nurturing to develop your character to its full potential.

Just Who Are You?

Keeping a reflective journal requires total honesty on your part. Don't try to make yourself appear better than you are, but by the same token, don't turn yourself into an ogre. You make choices in your life based on past experiences and your value system. The most important thing to remember is that you have options.

Once you determine the condition of your psyche—and, in turn, your character—you can reflect upon yourself and make changes to become a better person. Granted, some of your personality is determined by your genes, but environment plays a hefty role as well. You have the free will to choose. Now it's up to you to use it wisely.

A Method to the Madness

When you begin to keep a reflective journal, start with a thorough self-examination of your psyche to determine your strengths and weaknesses. Ask yourself a few questions about what you think and how you behave. Let me give you a list to get you started.

1. Do I often …
    a. Do things on impulse?
    b. Think about the consequences?

2. Do I think …
    a. Only about myself before I act?
    b. Most often about others before I act?

3. Do I often …
    a. Deviate from my value system?
    b. Live by my value system consistently?

4. Do I …
    a. Have to have immediate gratification?
    b. Find contentment in delaying gratification for the proper time and place?

5. Do I …
    a. Like to compete for the sheer enjoyment of competition?
    b. Enjoy competition because it motivates me to seek excellence?

6. Am I …
    a. Content to do only as much as necessary?
    b. Happy to try to do more than expected?

7. Do I …
    a. Lash out at someone who has done me a wrong?
    b. Walk away from someone who has wronged me with the intention of forgetting about it?

8. Do I …
    a. Hold a grudge?
    b. Forgive and forget?

If you answered "yes" to four or more A answers, you have a very well-developed id that is a bit more powerful than it should be. Others likely perceive you as a self-centered or snobbish person who has little or no concern for others.

If, on the other hand, you answered "yes" to four or more of the B answers, you probably have a well-developed superego. Others are apt to see you as an ethical person worthy of trust.

That's Not All, Folks

Use your reflective journal to write about other traits you have or wish you had. For example, if you know you're right about a certain point, are you willing to stand your ground? Or do you back down? Which action do you admire? Most people would say they admire the person who remains firm. Do you have the courage to do that?

Of course you do. You just have to find it.

If courage is a trait you wish to develop, then you should more thoroughly examine your superego. If yours is already well developed, you can remind yourself of your values and the principles you hold dear. Write about those values and look for ways to call upon your courage.

First Steps

Start small. You don't have to go out and save the world on your first attempt. It might be something as small as standing in line at the deli counter. The person behind the counter might ask, "What can I get for you?" You might not be the next person in line. If not, then courageously step forward and point to the person who is.

Yes, it is a very small step toward the development of your courage, but you should write about it in your journal and acknowledge your growth. The next time you face a slightly more important situation in which you must step forward, you can find your courage much more easily and do the right thing. And write about it. Congratulate yourself.

Don't discount these little steps. At first they may seem small and unimportant, but many small steps can take you a great distance. Small acts of courage lead to larger ones, the stuff that heroes are made of.

Other Struggles

Keeping a reflective journal necessarily means struggle, but we human creatures thrive on adversity. Adversity builds character, and that is, after all, your goal. You want your character to grow, to thrive, to blossom. Let me give you a list of some other traits you might wish to work on to develop your character:

➤ Perseverance
➤ Patience

➤ Forgiveness

➤ Spontaneity

➤ Light-heartedness

➤ Understanding

➤ Concern

➤ Thoughtfulness

➤ Inquisitiveness

➤ Empathy

➤ Scholarship

➤ Generosity

➤ Prudence

➤ Honor

➤ Virtue

By no means is this list complete. I'm sure if you sat down for about three minutes, you could think of many more, but you get the idea.

Making a List and Checking It Twice

As you make your list of desirable traits, honestly evaluate which ones you already have and which ones you'd like to develop. Record all this in your journal. Seeing it on paper somehow makes everything much more real. It also makes things easier to take hold of emotionally.

Then, one at a time, think of ways you can develop each characteristic. I'm sure you have opportunities in your life to show more generosity to others. Look for those chances and decide to take advantage of them. Take each trait in turn and do the same.

At the end of every day, write in your journal about how well you succeeded at each attempt, and congratulate yourself. If you failed that day, record that as well and vow to try harder next time. Never forget: You can do this.

Character Counts

Of all the aspects of ourselves that we present to the world, the one thing that counts most is character. At times, people may look the other way at transgressions against the accepted code of behavior while at the same time recognizing the wrongness of the action.

The reflective journal acts not only as a mirror of your inner self but as a means to improve the person it reflects. None of us is perfect. We all have lots of room for improvement. It's up to you to make the choice and take the action. Ask yourself: Can you be a better person in six months? Of course you can.

The Least You Need to Know

➤ You can determine the strengths and weaknesses of your character.

➤ You have the power to become a better person.

➤ Keeping a reflective journal can help you make choices in your life to blossom into the best person you can become.

➤ Character does count.

Chapter 12

The Spiritual Journal

There has been a resurgence of interest in spirituality in the past decade. People used to shy away from discussing the spiritual side of their lives, thinking they might offend people or make them feel uncomfortable. That's all changed. People now talk about spirituality openly, and along with the renewed interest in spirituality has come a change in its meaning. No longer connected to any one religion, we now think of spirituality as possible within *any* religious context as well as without any religion whatsoever.

If you're interested in exploring your spirituality, consider keeping a spiritual journal. Understanding that you can bare your soul without fear confers the freedom to delve into every corner of your heart to discover the good, the bad, and the ugly parts of yourself.

The Biggest Question of Them All

One of the main reasons people keep spiritual journals is to seek the answers to variations on a very important question:

➤ "Why am I here?"

➤ "What is my purpose in life?"

➤ "What is my connection to others?"

➤ "What will happen to me after I die?"

Any philosopher or theologian will tell you that some of the wisest people ever to have lived have pondered these questions. Don't let that keep you from seeking the answers yourself, though. It is often the search for the answer, and not necessarily the answer itself, that will bring you into closer touch with your spiritual side. In this chapter, I will show you how you can use your spiritual journal to help you attain your spiritual goals.

The Write Idea

God, Allah, Buddha, the divine, the natural world ... People have all sorts of names for the spiritual force in their lives. To avoid confusion, I will use "the divine," but feel free to substitute a more appropriate word that works for you as you read along!

Finding Your Spiritual Side

Spirituality may mean different things to different people. Let me suggest a few ways people may define it. You may recognize a definition that speaks to your idea of spirituality or these suggestions might spark a new idea for you.

➤ A better connection with the divine

➤ A better connection with nature

➤ Finding greater joy in life

➤ Finding satisfaction in helping others

➤ Having concern for doing the right thing rather than taking the expedient action

➤ Searching for peace of mind and soul

➤ Finding your reason for being

No matter how you choose to define spirituality for yourself, it is a concept that requires reflection in order to fully understand and attain. A journal, by now you have certainly figured out, is an ideal tool for reflecting on any number of things ... so why not your spirit self? As you can see, none of this has anything to do with any particular religion. Rather, it views mankind as having a connection to both the divine and nature. Keeping a spiritual journal helps you learn more about the spiritual side of yourself and how you connect with the world, both seen and unseen.

Listen Up!

How well you hear the voice of your spirit depends on how well you can sift through the clamor of everything else around you.

The voices of your children and spouse, friends, co-workers, and boss all probably demand your time and attention, leaving little, if any, time for you to listen to "the voice" of your spirit. It's important to set aside quiet time for yourself to write in your journal—no matter whether it's a goal-oriented log or a historical journal—but it's particularly important to make quiet time to write in your spiritual journal.

Quiet Time

Flip back to Chapter 4, "The Journaling Habit," for some ideas to help you find a good time to write in your journal. Remember, however, that you only need a few minutes away from everything and everybody. The soul, such a solitary entity, doesn't interact well with anyone but you and needs your undivided attention.

You may have a favorite place somewhere in your house, such as your bedroom, next to a window with a view, or a cozy corner in the kitchen. If you're an outdoors-type person, being close to nature might inspire you. Perhaps you have a favorite tree you could sit under, or take a walk in the park. You know best of all what touches your soul and what will excite your spirit.

Take a Deep Breath

Because your spiritual journal requires more quiet and introspection than most other diary types, be sure to give yourself permission to take the time and make the quiet you need. Before you begin each writing session, find a comfortable sitting position and close your eyes.

Take a deep breath and stretch your arms up over your head. Hold them high for a few seconds. Slowly exhale and lower your arms to your sides. Feel the motion of your body. Feel the breath going in and out of your lungs. Pay attention to the motion of your diaphragm. Repeat this exercise five to ten times.

This exercise will help you relieve stress and let your body and mind relax. Only when you are relaxed will you connect fully with your spiritual side.

Eyes Wide Shut

With your eyes still closed, take your pen in hand or place your fingers on the keyboard and sit quietly for several seconds. Look inside yourself. Listen to the thoughts and identify your spiritual

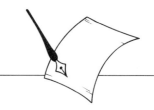

Putting Pen to Paper

For a spiritual journal, it's particularly important to choose a quiet corner where no one will bother you. Unplug the phones and hide yourself away for a short time to shut out the sounds and distractions of the material world. Give your inner voice the chance to be heard.

The Write Idea

If you need a little inspiration each day, keep a book on hand that offers daily suggestions for spiritual contemplation, such as *365 Days of Spiritual Growth* by Paul E. Miller and Phyllis Cole-Dai.

issues. If you've decided to keep a spiritual journal, you probably already have a good idea of what these are for you.

If not, let me offer a few suggestions to get you started. Feel free to write brief answers to the questions as you go along. You can take up the issues at length in your spiritual journal. As you continue on your spiritual journey, other questions will come to mind that you can address over time:

1. What kind of God or Creator do I believe in, if at all? Merciful? Vengeful? Compassionate? Flexible? Inflexible?

2. Why do I believe that I am connected to something larger than myself? Gratitude? Fear? Faith?

3. What can I do to improve myself spiritually?

4. How much do I really care about material things?

5. How can I use my growing spirituality to improve my relationships with the people in my life?

6. Are my goals in life tied to material or spiritual success?

7. How much of myself do I give in my relationships—both spiritual and personal?

Putting Pen to Paper

Don't interpret doubts about your spiritual side as weakness in your faith. Rather, use these doubts as a way to better understand yourself and your connection to the divine.

With these questions as a point of departure, you can take one at a time and write about it extensively. Listen to that tiny voice that struggles to be heard. Encourage it to shout instead of whisper, to be assertive instead of tentative, to function with confidence instead of trepidation.

One at a Time

As other spiritual questions and concerns come to mind, you can write them down on a separate page at the end of your book, make them part of your daily entry, or keep a separate notebook for them. But keep track of these questions.

Putting Pen to Paper

Welcome each new test of faith. Each challenge only serves to strengthen us.

The fact that you thought of them at all means your soul has concerns, and you should address them. Don't depend on yourself to remember such an important list without writing it down. As you begin to address your list of concerns, you may benefit from reading what others have written about them. They can give you a different perspective to consider.

I encourage you to read books about spiritual issues. Other perspectives will give you ideas to consider and write about. After all, we were endowed with intellects so that we might question and seek the truth.

Going by the Book— the Holy Book

You might also consider beginning each journal-writing period by reading an excerpt from a sacred book. Each religion has its own holy writings, which serve as the foundation for its beliefs. If you are truly eclectic and ecumenical in your tastes, you may have a copy of several of these books close at hand. For example, you might have a copy of the Bible, the Talmud, the Koran, and Buddhist scripture on your bookshelf. You might also consider reading books about the natural world.

The Write Idea

An interesting book that takes a slightly different, yet traditional, approach to spirituality is *9½ Mystics: The Kabbala Today* by Herbert Weiner, Elie Wiesel, and Adin Steinsaltz.

When it's time to write in your journal, pick one of these books and find a short quotation—either at random or one that you find particularly interesting. Write it in your journal and then contemplate not only its meaning but its significance to you as an individual. Think about how its wisdom can help you grow.

Here are some questions to help get you started:

1. What might this quote mean?
2. What lesson might the person who wrote this have wanted me to take from it?
3. Is this quote meaningful to me? If so, why?

Putting Pen to Paper

As a person of faith, you likely believe that a higher being plays a major role in your life, and you may revere the wisdom of scripture. Recognize this scripture as one of the ways that can help you connect better with the divine as well as with others.

Perhaps the excerpt you chose to write about wasn't as random as you thought. Maybe you were guided to it by some larger, more powerful force that knew you could benefit from that particular concept. For people of certain faiths, the idea that God or the divine would take such a personal interest in an individual is not only comforting but fundamental. When such things seem to happen, I encourage you to write about them and how they affect you.

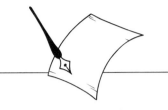

Putting Pen to Paper

Getting in touch with your soul may prove difficult at first. Get some ideas from Roger Walsh's *Essential Spirituality: The 7 Central Practices to Awaken Heart and Mind.*

The Write Idea

Early church mystics developed their spirituality through a combination of meditation, contemplation, and prayer.

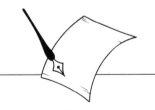

Putting Pen to Paper

Try reading *The Complete Idiot's Guide to Awakening Your Spirituality* by Jonathan Robinson. It offers great suggestions to the novice as well as the veteran.

Synchronicity

Have you ever encountered a fact, a song, a person, or an item that you haven't thought about in years? It may even be a totally new concept for you. You react with a shrug, shake it off, and then move on. Then a day or two later, you notice some reference to it again. Some call it coincidence. A person with a spiritual mindset would call it synchronicity.

Look for these occurrences in your life. Consider that perhaps you were meant to know the facts or experience the events for some particular reason to aid you in your spiritual journey. When they do occur, pursue them. Why suddenly do you see and hear references from various and independent sources about the problem of hunger? Maybe you should get involved with the local food bank.

Discuss the possibilities in your journal and explore the idea that this series of events or facts may have a lesson to teach you. Maybe your soul recognizes this as a way to help others. Such reflections can help you hear more readily what your soul has to tell you.

Simple Gifts

As you become more acquainted with your spirit, you may feel that meditation will yield some very real benefits, among them stress reduction and increased self-awareness. Of all the benefits, however, an increased connection to your soul—and, in turn, God—is probably the biggest and most important.

How you choose to meditate is entirely up to you, and I hope you will pursue mediation for a number of reasons. You can find a variety of books on the subject that can provide you with suggestions on how to begin and how to develop your abilities and spirituality.

Take the lessons from your meditation and write about them. Learn how you can put them to work in your life to blossom into a better person, someone who contributes to his or her family and community. Develop your compassion, patience, and ability to bear up under the struggles that life sends your way.

A Clear Path

Once you've learned to shut out the noise around you and reduce your stress, close your eyes and listen to what your soul has to tell you. Think about your attitudes, opinions, and behavior. Contemplate the things that motivate you to act, all in relation to a particular aspect of your life.

Remember that, although you're on a journey within yourself, your object is to expand your spirituality in the context of the divine and the people around you. None of us exists in a vacuum, and it serves no good to discover yourself without the benefit of knowing how you fit into the greater scheme of things.

Mission Possible

During the course of keeping a spiritual journal, you might pursue a very important question: What is my mission in life? What is my reason for being here? It may or may not be tied to a talent you have. For example, if you have the gift of public speaking, perhaps you were meant to speak out on certain issues.

To discover your mission, look for everyday opportunities to act, to reach out and do some good. Does it seem to you that certain themes keep repeating themselves? For example, if you often find yourself in situations in which people need your help in a certain area, that might be a hint.

Whenever you feel drawn to a particular area, don't forget to write about it in your journal. We are necessarily selective about what we include in our journals (we can't write about everything, can we?), though the selection process might not be a conscious activity. You might just find that, without meaning to, you have written about some particular activity or idea several times. Perhaps this is an area you should explore further as a mission in your life.

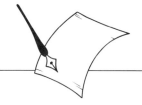

Putting Pen to Paper

For most of us, the path to spirituality is a difficult process because we strive for perfection. While a commendable goal, you have to know it's not achievable. For encouragement and a dose of reality, take a look at *The Spirituality of Imperfection: Storytelling and the Journey to Wholeness* by Earnest Kurtz and Katherine Ketcham.

The Write Idea

Some of history's most spiritual people sought and discovered an overriding reason for their life and pursued that mission with a passion. People such as St. Francis of Assisi, Mahatma Gandhi, and St. Joan of Arc knew with a certainty what they had to do, and did it.

The Write Idea

In a recent survey, 92 percent of Americans acknowledged their belief in a supreme being.

Another Spiritual Book

We've already considered how you can use your journal and spiritual books such as the Bible and the Koran to help you understand your spiritual side, but there's one more book you should study carefully: your spiritual journal.

After you've written in your spiritual journal for a few weeks, just think what a fascinating portrait of your inner life—your soul—you will have painted. Be sure to take the time every few weeks to return to what you've already written in your spiritual journal. This can help you better understand where you are spiritually and where you want to go. The sky is the limit!

The Least You Need to Know

➤ Spirituality does not necessarily mean adherence to any particular religion.

➤ Keeping a spiritual journal is one way to examine your soul and your relationship with others in your life.

➤ Prayer, meditation, and contemplation all work to expand your soul. Keeping a journal is an expression of that growth.

➤ In a quiet spot, you can hear your soul.

➤ With a spiritual journal, you can discover your mission in life.

Chapter 13

The Family Journal

In This Chapter

➤ Making a family commitment to keep a journal

➤ How everyone can participate

➤ Getting creative and having some fun

➤ Using the journal as a bonding tool

➤ Keeping your treasured memories

Of all the different types of journals, I think the family journal is the most fun because everyone can participate in some way. Yes, with a little creativity, even infants can contribute. Whether your family consists of 2 or 20 makes no difference. The time you spend apart and the time you spend alone is all subject matter for the family journal.

It can bring you together at the end of the day or at the end of the week. Just think of the good times you can laugh about as you relate the funny things that happened to one another. And consider the lessons everyone can learn as you share the more serious moments.

The family journal also will become a family treasure in years to come after the children have grown and gone their separate ways. Trust me. I know from experience.

Knock, Knock

On the day you begin your own family with that very special person, an exceptional opportunity knocks at your door. Now that you have made the commitment to share your life with someone else, this pledge brings you closer to that person than anyone else.

Words of Wisdom

"The palest ink is better than the best memory."

—Chinese proverb

This should be your most intimate friend, the person with whom you share everything—from how your day at work went and how you feel about local politicians to your deepest, most spiritual thoughts. The discussions you have can become material for your family journal.

If you haven't taken advantage of keeping a family journal from the very beginning of your relationship, take heart. You can start your family journal at any point. You can begin with memories to play "catch up," or you can just make today's events the first entry. It's entirely up to you. But I'll bet that memories will creep in from time to time in the future.

Putting Pen to Paper

When working on your journal with your partner, choose a type of music that you both like to play. You'll notice that certain types of music may influence the choices you make about what to write. Play with this phenomenon. Try classical music, rock 'n' roll, jazz, blues, and whatever other types you have on hand.

New Commitments

At the beginning of your new life together, decide whether you'd like to keep your journal using a book and pen or a computer. Both options have pros and cons, but most families prefer to use a book and pen because you can pass them from person to person.

Next decide on your writing schedule. Every day is ideal, but many families feel that once a week is sufficient, mainly because work, school, church, and other activities make it difficult to get everyone together every day. If you opt for the weekly gathering, I suggest you make it a priority. Schedule everything else after your family journaling time.

Discuss all the options and make decisions together. A joint decision will be easier to comply with than if just one of you makes it. For some tips on times that might be the most convenient, refer to Chapters 3, "Begin at the Beginning," and 4, "The Journaling Habit." In any case, make the commitment and keep it.

Decide together what you'll include in that day's entry. Spend time talking about it. Identify the humor, sadness, and emotion in the events. Then together, write about them as they happened, each of you adding your own unique insights. In years to come, you'll look back with fondness, not only on the events you recorded but on the time you spent together.

Family Additions

If and when you add children to your family, you can use your family journal to record your emotions as you learn about the pregnancy, prepare for the birth, and welcome the new child into your family. The family journal can also be used as a tool to help you prepare for the arrival of the baby. You can discuss nursery preparations, what baby books you have read or those you want to read, and the supplies you need or have already purchased. This will be a wonderful record to look back on after the child has grown.

After the baby arrives, you and your spouse can use the journal to record the experiences of being new parents. You can describe how it felt to hold that tiny new life in your hands for the first time. You can record the many "firsts"—such as the first full night of sleep, first words, first steps—that your baby will achieve. Along with the many thrills and emotional highs, you can write about the "lows" in your journal as well: how tired you were after the baby kept you up all night, what kind of adjustments you needed to make to your lifestyle after the baby was born. When your child is older, just think how wonderful it will be for him or her to read about these precious moments!

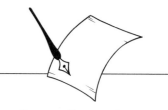

Putting Pen to Paper

The family journal is an ideal place to write about the firsts as well as other events in your child's life such as immunizations, childhood diseases, and funny or poignant moments.

The Write Idea

New babies often become the focus of your journal. This is only natural, and over time you'll eventually write with more balance—returning to discussions of other family members and events. Meanwhile, go with the flow and have fun with it.

As Time Goes By

You will watch in wonder as your children grow from toddlers into young children, teens, and finally, adults, and you can record your impressions and emotions in your family journal. What wonderful things you can relate about their development as they emerge into beautiful individuals with endless possibilities before them.

Everyone Can Play

Every member of the family can participate in some way in the family journal, even infants. Get creative and use the journal as a way to nurture a sense of belonging in each person you count among your family community.

Cultivating this sense of belonging reinforces the bonding process, particularly among the very young, a very important consideration in their development. As the bonding continues, the child's sphere of concern expands, and his focus changes from total absorption in self to concern for others.

Putting Pen to Paper

View the journal as a way to teach your children the value of family.

Circulate the journal among everyone in the family and have them write something about their day; a sentence or two should suffice. Then ask each person to read aloud what he or she has written.

In a similar manner, older children and even adults will reap positive benefits from the family journal. As they share the things they've experienced, the closeness within the family grows. The times you spend together writing in the journal and laughing are irreplaceable and priceless.

You Must Have Been a Beautiful Baby

That squirming little bundle in your arms is a miracle that screams to let you know its wants and needs. As a parent, you recognize the different cries. You know immediately when the baby needs changing, is hungry, needs a nap, or just needs someone to play with and cuddle with. Despite their lack of language skills, even this smallest member of the family can participate in drawing your family closer together.

While you sit and write in your family diary, hold the baby close and explain what you're writing. Of course, an infant won't understand a single word you say, but they will understand your smile and your pleasant manner. Make this a most enjoyable time for your baby.

Gently place their hand on the page and let them run their fingers across its surface. Let them experience the feel of paper. Say something like, "I'm writing all about you on this page, and when you get older you'll be able to read it for yourself." Don't talk baby talk, but do speak with a smile in your voice.

Place a crayon in the child's fist and let them make marks on the page. Tell them what a good baby they are and cuddle them.

If you have other children, encourage them to make conversation with the baby and cuddle. In fact, you should try to give the baby the impression that this entire activity revolves around them, as though they needed any further inducement in that direction. But your baby will grow in the knowledge that they are part of something bigger than themselves.

It's Toddler Time

As you know if you have a toddler, it's sometimes difficult to include them in family activities. With a little creativity and patience, however, you can involve them in the family journal.

When it's your toddler's turn to contribute to the journal, ask the child what he or she would like to put in the journal and explain that you will help.

Perhaps you can tell your child that you will begin to write what she'd like and then she can finish it. Even though most children have not yet mastered the art of writing at this age, they think they can. They try writing with a pencil or crayon every chance they get.

After you have written her entry, hand her a crayon and ask her to "write" something in the journal. When she has finished, complete it with a short note beneath the artwork that notes name of the author and the date. Your child will beam with pride, belonging, and a growing feeling of self-worth.

The Write Idea

If family entries mention your toddler, he or she will look forward to family journal time very much.

Young Children

As children mature and develop their language skills, their interest in the family journal will grow as well. In fact, they may want to write in the book themselves without any help from you. As you pass the book around at these gatherings, let the younger children take their turn. Coach them carefully and patiently about what to write and even how to form the letters if they need help. Keep it simple. Don't let them get frustrated or sit for long minutes without writing.

Help. Guide. Suggest. Even tell them what to write at first, perhaps just their name. And when they have made their entry, praise them. Nothing breeds success like success, and you definitely want them to succeed in this family exercise.

With each entry your child makes, you can teach grammar, punctuation, spelling, and vocabulary but in a positive way. Let me give you an example.

Suppose your child wrote, "I like getting things for my birthday."

You should ask, "What kinds of things?" with the thought of getting the child to be more precise with his language. Instead of "things," encourage him to write "gifts" or "presents." The child already knows those words, but by encouraging him to use more variety in his writing, you will be teaching a skill that will last a lifetime.

Time to Be Cool

Of all age groups, teens may pose the greatest challenge to participation in the family journal. Busy with school, sports, friends, and other activities, some decide that, at this time in their lives, they'd rather be anywhere else than with their family.

Take heart.

Know that you are not alone. The reasons are too numerous and complex to explain here, but it's a normal part of life. The gap between the generations is never more noticeable than when you have teenagers in the house.

Eventually, your teenagers will likely announce that they're "too cool" for the family journal and that they'd rather be with their friends. Don't fret. Don't fume. Don't fight about it. Communicate your respect for their desires to be elsewhere or to do other things, but remind them that this is something the family does together and that it only takes a short time. You can also compromise on the issue.

The Write Idea

Put your teens in charge of background music for journal-writing time. They'll have something they truly enjoy while you have them at this important family activity. You may not love the music, but you can't have everything.

Give a Little

No matter how important the family journal is, your family relationships are far more important. Don't be inflexible. Offer to make some changes to accommodate your teen.

If you have instituted a curfew, a time at which your teen has to be home anyway, change your journal time to coincide with that time. Another tactic you could use, particularly if your teen enjoys eating, would be to change journal writing time to just before or after dinner. The family should have dinner together at least once a week anyway. Take advantage of the fact that everyone is there.

If your teen enjoys certain privileges, explain that privileges come with responsibilities and that journal participation is a responsibility. Instead of meeting every evening, perhaps a weekly schedule would work better for all concerned at this time in your life.

You could find other ways to compromise as well. Ask your teens to voice their objections and then work together to address them. Maybe they think the amount of time devoted to the journal is overly long. Agree to shorten it. There is any number of alternatives. Look at all the options together and find one that everyone can live with.

Another tactic would be to have your teen invite a friend from time to time for dinner and include the friend in the family journal time afterward.

If nothing works and your teen continues to balk at participating in the family journal, maybe it's time to give in and enjoy your family journal without your teen. Be assured that when he grows into an adult, he will want to rejoin the family in writing in this family activity.

Expanding Your Family Circle

While the focus of your family journal will be your nuclear family, feel free to include other members of your family who live outside your home as well as close friends. Grandparents, aunts, uncles, cousins, and friends all influence us in one way or another. Write about them as well.

If they happen to be visiting during your family journal time, invite them to participate and make a note in your journal that you have a "guest" present. That short note will bring a rich memory to mind in times to come.

As you pass the journal from one person to the next, give your guest the opportunity to contribute. In fact, to honor your guest, you could make him the star of that day's entry. Let everyone in the family make a comment about the honored guest, perhaps telling him what a wonderful friend or relative he is.

From the Past

Who hasn't experienced the loss of loved ones? No matter how many years pass, we still miss them. Sometimes the anniversary of their death or their birthday brings them to mind more acutely. Once more, we may feel the pain of their passing and wish they could be with us again.

On that day, why not make that particular person the focus of your family journal? Let each family member write a short note telling how much they miss her, how they wish they could have shared a special experience with her, or describing a special memory they have of her.

Out of the Ordinary

While most of your journal entries will include the everyday things, you can spice it up by including those special occasions like holidays, birthdays, anniversaries, parties, special awards, and other events of note.

Also, why not include family photos, drawings, and newspaper clippings in your journal? All of those little extra items will add depth and character to your journal and increase its value as a treasure of memories in years to come.

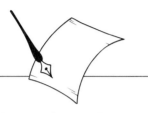

Putting Pen to Paper

Don't forget to include your pets as well. Many of us consider them a part of the family. Wouldn't it be fun to place a paw print in the pages of your journal?

Drawing the Family Together

In these days in which every member of the family has so much to do and so many places to go, finding time to spend together can be difficult, but it can also be precious.

Because we spend so much time apart, a family journal is an ideal way to keep the lines of communication open among family members. It's also a great way to make sure the family spends at least a little time together.

This is your family, the people you care about more than anyone else on this earth. You want to engender loving, caring, selfless relationships among all your family members. Everyday life presents us with ways to do that. Although a journal is only one way to achieve that closeness, it is a very valuable tool.

The Least You Need to Know

➤ A family journal is a fun and easy way to stay connected with your family.

➤ Everyone in the family—even infants—can participate in the family journal.

➤ Consider including extended family members and dear friends.

➤ A family journal can be used to memorialize loved ones who have died.

➤ Include the little extras like photos and newspaper clippings in your journal.

Chapter 14

The Dream Journal

In This Chapter

➤ What we learn from night dreams

➤ Learning the secrets of the heart from daydreams

➤ Interpreting what your dreams mean

➤ Visualizing your way to your heart's desire

➤ Making your dreams come true

Our dreams, whether they come from nighttime machinations of the mind or day-time imaginings, all come from somewhere in our psyche. They don't have to obey the laws of physics. They don't have to make sense, and best of all, we can do the impossible in our dreams.

Raise your hand if you've ever seen yourself flying like a bird in one of your dreams. Of course you have. We all have at one time or another. And have you ever told the schoolyard bully exactly what you thought of him and escaped unscathed?

This is the stuff of which dreams are made: the impossible, the unlikely, the terrifying. And although on the surface they seem to make no sense at all, if we look at them more closely, we can find a grain of truth to build on and make some other dreams come true.

The Nature of Dreams

We dream when we sleep, but we don't know exactly why. Despite all the research on dreams (and believe me, there has been a lot of it!), scientists can't answer all of our questions about dreams. One thing scientists do know is that, without sleep for extended periods, we'd probably go insane. And listen to this: Those same scientists have determined that losing touch with reality comes not so much from lack of sleep but rather the lack of dreams!

Maybe the brain works like a personal computer. Periodically, we have to defrag our hard drives; otherwise, the data will become so jumbled that our computers slow to a crawl. Dreams might serve the same purpose, reorganizing all of our sensory data, all the experiences we have had, and all the things we thought about in any given day. This might help explain why, when we think a great deal about something, we often dream about it.

Whatever the reason we dream, whatever the purpose our dreams serve, if we spend some time thinking about them, we might learn a little bit about ourselves.

As the product of the subconscious mind, our dreams could prove significant in a number of ways, from getting to the source of an irritability to improving a relationship. What you see within the realm of dreams might surprise you and at the same time give you a reason to consider something previously thought impossible.

Whether they are daydreams or images that visit you in the night, dreams hold the key to some of our deepest thoughts and desires. By keeping a dream journal, you give yourself the opportunity to bring those shadowy concepts out into the open for examination. Writing your dreams down enables you to take a closer look at the things that truly concern you.

With a dream journal you can note patterns or recurring themes and then take the time to consider what they mean. Should you seek a new job? Should you commit to that special someone? Should you relocate? Is this really what you'd rather be doing? You may be able to answer those questions and more once you know what your dreams are trying to tell you.

Do You Dream?

I'm sure you know people who say they never dream. These people are probably wrong because scientists who specialize in sleep research have found that, with rare exceptions in cases of severe brain dysfunction, we all dream every night. It's just that some people may not remember their dreams once they wake up. If you're one of those unlucky people, a dream journal is probably not right for you!

In fact, scientists have found that we may have several dreams in a single night. A single theme may run through all of them, or they may each treat a different subject.

Paper Dreams

As soon as you wake up from a dream, even if it's in the middle of the night, write down what you remember in a small dream journal that you keep by the bed. Even if you only remember a few points or only some people from the dream, the information could prove useful when you try to interpret it.

Don't leave out the details if you can remember them, no matter how insignificant they might appear. Like detectives who ask for every small detail from the people they interview, try to remember everything. Was the sweater in your dream blue or was it red? If you remember, write it down. It's the details that might help you make sense of an otherwise meaningless dream.

Dream Interpretation

Many methods for dream interpretation exist, from the Freudian to the whimsical. You can find any number of books on the subject, each written with a different philosophy in mind. Some books concentrate on scientific or psychological research; others discuss philosophy or metaphysics. I encourage you to look through several at the bookstore and decide which one suits you best.

From among the different choices, find a comfortable approach that fits your personality. Once

The Write Idea

Some Native American cultures believe that dreams open the door to the spirit world and that the spirits communicate with us through our dreams. During their visits, they may pass on knowledge or point us in a certain direction. Many other cultures throughout history have viewed dreams and their interpretation as important for a variety of purposes.

Putting Pen to Paper

Don't rely on your middle-of-the-night memory to recall your dream in the morning. Write it down during the night, even if you have to scrawl something in the dark.

117

The Write Idea

Don't be disappointed if the first method of dream interpretation doesn't seem to work for you. Try another and give yourself some time to practice.

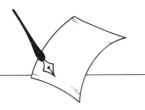

Putting Pen to Paper

A few popular books on the subject of interpreting dreams include *The Hidden Power of Dreams* by Denise Linn; *The Complete Idiot's Guide to Interpreting Your Dreams* by Marci Pliskin and Shari L. Just; *The Dream Book: Symbols for Self-Understanding* by Betty Bethards; and *Awakening the Real You: Awareness Through Dreams and Intuition* by Nancy C. Pohle and Ellen L. Selover.

you've settled on a particular book, buy it and keep it with your dream journal. You'll want it close at hand for a reference when you write about your dreams in your diary.

Common Interpretations

Although many approaches to dream interpretation exist, many share some common ground. The following are some fairly common explanations:

➤ Flying—Desire for freedom

➤ Losing teeth or other body parts—Fear of losing a loved one

➤ Someone who has died—Need to resolve certain issues or communicate something to them

➤ Slow-motion running—Trying to reach a goal that always seems out of reach

➤ Appearing naked before people—Feeling of vulnerability

➤ Wandering aimlessly—Lack of a goal

➤ Being chased—Feeling of being overwhelmed by a problem

As you look down this list, you'll likely recognize at least one or two dreams you've had, and I think you'll see a certain logic to these interpretations. These should get you started, but of course, books devoted to the subject can give you more suggestions.

Follow the Yellow Brick Road

Just as Dorothy followed the yellow brick road to reach the Emerald City and the Wizard of Oz on her homeward journey, you too need to follow a certain path to understand your dreams. The following process can serve as a guide on your journey to Oz.

Write It Down

The first step is to write down your dream in vivid detail. Try not to leave anything out. I realize that, if you made some quick notes in the middle of the night, your record will be far from complete, but it may be enough to take you through the process.

Make the Connection with Reality

Once you've recorded your dream, ask yourself why you dreamed of this particular person, situation, or thing. Did something similar happen to you in the last day or two? Did you meet this person recently? Does this dream even vaguely resemble anything currently going on in your life? Reach for an explanation if you have to. As important as they are to our existence, dreams are not easy to analyze. Write all of your ideas down.

If you find an explanation that fits with something going on in your life, then you can easily explain the dream. If nothing comes to mind, however, try to think of some possibilities and record them in your journal as things to think about. On the other hand, if you see a relationship between your dream and real life, try to explain that relationship and your dream.

Look for Hidden Desires

If life seems to be a jumble sometimes, imagine how our dreams appear. For starters, try to keep things simple and logical when you try to explain your dreams. For example, if you dreamed about a co-worker in a romantic way, maybe it's because you harbor affection for that person.

Did you dream about a new car? If so, have you been considering buying a new vehicle? Did you dream about your house going up in flames? Perhaps you know you have so many repairs to make that, on some level, you feel it would be easier to burn the place down and start from scratch. Did you dream about an ocean cruise? Maybe you've always harbored a secret desire for such a voyage.

You can do this. Look at your dream and decide how it relates to your life.

Deciding Whether to Act

Once you understand what your dream has to do with your life, you can take a look at that desire or experience and decide whether you want to pursue it. Of course, you have to ask yourself if it's appropriate. If it's not, accept the feelings for what they are and take no action. If action is appropriate, then by all means do something. Surprisingly, it might be something you would never have thought of if you had not kept track of your dreams. Bon voyage!

Putting Pen to Paper

If you have frequent nightmares, look carefully at your life and at any unresolved issues you may have. You may benefit from keeping a diary that merges the features of the dream journal with the cathartic or unsent letter journal.

Figuring Out the Fears

Most psychologists agree that dreams come from unresolved issues, ongoing situations that have not yet come to a satisfactory conclusion. We either think about them on a conscious level or allow our subconscious to carry the burden. One way or the other, they occupy part of our thought processes and surface in our dreams.

In any case, we probably find the situation threatening in some way, and it makes us uneasy. Think of all the exams you took in school. Consider projects at work for which you are responsible. What about having to stand up in front of a group of people to make a presentation? All of these situations cause a certain amount of anxiety, and the best we can do is see them through and dream about them.

Lions and Tigers and Bears, Oh My!

Let me give you a simple example. A young child visiting the zoo may find the experience totally enjoyable until he comes upon the great cats. The sheer enormity of the animals may astound him but not frighten him. And then, one huge tiger suddenly turns in the direction of the child and roars. The frightened child will likely scream and cry until the parent scoops the child away and rushes out of earshot.

On the way home, the child may dwell on that one encounter, nearly forgetting every other happy experience of the day. That roaring tiger will loom larger than life in his mind, and the fear will not go away. That night, the child may very well have a nightmare and wake up screaming because a tiger was roaring and chasing him. In this example, fear is the unresolved issue. From time to time, the child may have nightmares about being chased by a tiger until he realizes that the danger was never real and the experience is over.

The Write Idea

Science and philosophy both adhere to the rule known as Ockham's razor, or the Law of Parsimony. It states that "Entities should not be multiplied needlessly." In other words, when presented with two or more theories to explain something, the simplest is usually the preferable. In addition, it says that you should first attempt to explain things in terms of what you already know. I suggest you use Ockham's razor when you interpret your dreams.

In some instances, depending on the child's personality and age, he might stand up to the tiger in his nightmare, perhaps even striking back and sending the tiger packing. In choosing to stand, fight, and win, the child will likely eliminate any further tiger nightmares because he worked through the fear.

Pass the Cigar, Please

If you decide to spend some time seriously interpreting your dreams (that is, getting below the surface to find deeper reasons), remember to keep things in perspective. Granted, the answer to a recurring dream may lie in some obscure and long-forgotten experience, but consider the simplest and most logical explanation first. Remember, "Sometimes a cigar is just a cigar."

Finding a Pattern

When you record your dreams over a period of time, look for patterns, recurrent themes, or particular people or events that you dream about regularly. Here are a few questions to help you analyze your life and your dreams:

1. Do you have to right a wrong?
2. Should you call that person you haven't talked to in months?
3. Do you need to complete some task?
4. Have you forgotten to do something that you had promised you would do?
5. How significant was/is this person in your life?
6. How significant was/is this event in your life?
7. Do you need to tell this person how you feel about him or her?

These questions will lead you to others and will help you figure out what your subconscious mind thinks is important.

New Directions

It might also surprise you to find that your mind keeps pointing you in another direction either professionally or personally. For example, if you've had the same job for a period of time, you might be thinking about moving on to something else. Do you dream about other careers? Do you dream about one in particular? Would you prefer to move to that job track? Only you can say for certain.

Pay attention to your dreams. After all, they come from a part of the brain that we can't access at will. Look and listen to what your dreams have to tell you about yourself and your life.

A Little Bit of Night at Noon

"Stop your daydreaming. Pay attention!"

I can still hear my teacher trying to get my attention on a beautiful spring day. I don't suppose you could blame me. I was only eight years old, and the warm day, awash in sunshine, was a welcome change from the long, cold winter.

As we grow up, some of us leave that fantasy life behind, but some of us hold on to it and find that it enriches our life.

Hopes and Dreams

If you happen to be a daydreamer, you most likely have a vivid and active imagination. Don't hide it. Instead, congratulate yourself on your talent and take advantage of it because your daydreams reveal your deepest desires.

If you are a daydreamer, I suggest you keep a journal to record your fantasies. As with your nighttime dreams, take note of any patterns or recurring fantasies. Although they are a mixture of imagination, reality, and the subconscious, they can shed some light on the hopes and dreams you hold most dear.

Don't Hide from Your Daydreams

No matter how you may deny it on a conscious level, your daydreams might reveal that you'd like to have a relationship with a particular person or make a move to obtain a different job. Pay attention to what your daydreams are trying to tell you.

As you write about them in your journal, consider and record the possibilities as well. New jobs, new relationships, new houses, new cars, and new directions for your life can all have their beginnings in your daydreams.

Visualization

I once had a client who created hand-painted designs on clothing. She confided to me that, for many years, she kept a dream journal in which she wrote down all the things she wanted to accomplish. She said that keeping such a journal had helped her achieve her goals.

She's not alone in her belief. A number of psychologists suggest visualization to their patients as a means to help them achieve some goal. It's a healthy way to sort out the details of any goal you wish to achieve. The simple method involves three steps.

Imagine Reaching Your Goal

First, visualize what you want and add all the detail you can. Imagine yourself actually doing what you want: accepting the award you wish for, signing that contract, or marrying the person of your dreams. See yourself in your mind's eye doing the thing you desire. Then write about it in all its glory in your journal. As you describe it, allow yourself to feel all the emotions that go along with it.

Write about it for days or weeks if you like. Take it to the extreme—until you have memorized it and emblazoned it in your soul. When you have nothing new to say about your heart's desire, it's time to move on to the second step.

Running the Gauntlet

Next, imagine yourself going through all the things you need to do to reach your goal. That might include taking classes, practicing a piece of music, or gathering information for that all-important presentation at work. Write each step down in the order you'd have to do it.

The Write Idea

Tackling any goal in little steps makes it seem like less of a task, even those that would otherwise overwhelm us.

Visualize yourself doing all those things as clearly as if they were on your TV screen. When you have "seen" yourself go through all the paces to reach the goal, describe it all in your dream journal, complete with all the emotions you can imagine yourself feeling.

Turning Words into Actions

Once you've written down your goal and how you'll get there, spend a few moments each day rereading the initial journal entry regarding your current goal. You know what steps you have to take to achieve it, so ask yourself what you did today.

Did you call someone for information? Did you fill out any forms? Did you talk to someone who could help you get there? Whatever it was, write it down and track your progress. Each day, take another step to achieve your heart's desire.

If you accomplished something, by all means, congratulate yourself and plan out your next step. If you didn't move a step closer to your goal, then promise yourself to do better tomorrow and write down exactly what action you will take. Working toward a goal is the only way to get there. If it's a dream you have, put your dream journal to work for you.

Making Dreams Come True

Our dreams, whether they come to us at night, at noon, or from our imaginings, tell us something about ourselves. They reveal to us our failings as well as our strengths. They can point us in another direction or show us how to aim for another star. With the help of our dream journal, we can remember, interpret, and follow our dreams.

The Least You Need to Know

➤ Night dreams can reveal things that your subconscious thinks are important.

➤ Daydreams can show you where your hopes lie.

➤ Visualization can help you achieve your goals.

➤ You can use your dream journal to help you make your dreams come true.

Ye
olde
Historian

The Historical Journal

As far as I know, no one has invented a time machine. Nope, you can't go back in time to start all over again. You can't go back and record all of your experiences. And you can't go back to relive precious moments. You're stuck in the here and now with the rest of us. However, you can begin to keep an historical journal, a diary that re-captures past events of your life, much like a memoir but far less structured.

Your historical journal is the perfect place to record some very special stories, memories, and anecdotes that would otherwise disappear into the mists of time.

No Secondhand Rose

Now, like me and millions of others, you may wish you had gotten an earlier start on journal writing. It's not too late. If anything, because of the passage of time, you can bring a different perspective to your journal. Your firsthand memories are precious.

You witnessed the incidents and participated in the events. You felt the emotions and reacted. Just think how valuable your descriptions of a time long ago will be to your descendants and, yes, even historians. Your eyewitness accounts of your time and place in the world will prove valuable many years from now.

Peeking in the Window

You might wonder why anyone would care about your memories. You might ask, "Who would want to know what it was like to milk a cow by hand?" Before you answer your question with "Nobody," think about it: Wouldn't you like to read a diary of the day-to-day life of your great-grandmother and great-grandfather? I certainly would want to know how they went to the well each morning to fetch water or how long it took them to get to town riding in a wagon. You probably would, too. Not only because they were your grandparents, but because their words would give you a peek into another time and place.

Humans are voyeurs at heart. Consider, for example, how popular memoirs are—they flood the bestseller lists and our local bookstore's bookshelves. And our thirst for nonfiction and documentary books and movies about other people's lives has never been greater. So go ahead, leave your descendants a treasure: the true story of your life—told in your own words.

Words of Wisdom

"God gave us memory so that we might have roses in December."

–J. M. Barrie

The Write Idea

As a French word, *memoir* translates literally into English as "memory." Yet, as with many literal translations, "memory" doesn't convey the heart—the true meaning—of the word. Heart actually has a lot to do with *memoir*—perhaps "heartfelt memory" would be better.

Smelling the Roses

The fact that we can recollect incidents from 20, 30, 50, or more years ago means that they made a deep impression on us. In many instances, they left such a strong mark that, if we close our eyes, we can almost relive the event. We can hear the music, smell the roses, feel the smoothness of that new car's fender. So much more than memories, this is the stuff memoirs are made of. And each of these sensations carries with it an equally vivid memory, a story to tell.

So when you consider which stories to relate in your historical journal, pick those that have moved you, that have taught you something, or that have made some difference in your life, no matter how small.

Why Not Just Write an Autobiography?

So why shouldn't you just write an autobiography instead of keeping an historical journal? They sure sound a lot alike! Writing an autobiography is certainly an option to consider, but historical journals have a couple of advantages over autobiographies that you should know about before making your decision. When you keep an historical journal …

➤ You don't have to have a whole plan in place about what you want to write. You can start from whatever memory you think of first, write about it for a while, and then move on to an entirely different memory the next day. It doesn't matter what path your historical journal takes because you're not attempting to tell a book-length, coherent story of your life; rather, you're recording memories and events from your past.

➤ You don't have to worry about how to organize your memories. In other words, you don't have to follow a certain chronology, and you don't have to write about certain times and events if you don't want to or can't remember them very well. Today you might decide to write about something that happened to you in the fifth grade; tomorrow you might record a memory from preschool. That's okay! You can include a snippet here and a snippet there with no worry about order or plot!

With so many other things to worry about in life, your journal certainly shouldn't cause you stress. On the contrary, your journal should offer you a respite from worry.

A Stumblefest

I can guarantee that, once you start to think about your past, your mind will recall one event after another. It will happen so quickly that it will seem as though your memories are tripping over each other inside your brain, all fighting to get out. Now that paints a picture!

But really, that's what will happen. One memory begets another, and that stirs up another, and that gives birth to still another, *ad infinitum*—often more than you can handle. Although the brain functions in marvelous ways, we do tend to forget things, so you'll need to employ a method to help you keep a hold on all those wonderful memories once they come surging back.

Please, Take a Number!

As you continue to recall the events of your life, don't let them overwhelm you. Instead, take control of them by listing them in a memory notebook. Diarists who keep historical journals often record their ideas and memories in a small

Putting Pen to Paper

For your memory notebook, buy a notebook that's small enough to fit in a pocket or purse so you can carry it with you anywhere. That way, whenever a memory pops into your mind, you can jot it down right then.

notebook that I like to call a memory notebook. They can always refer to this notebook when they need to pick the next memory to write about.

The memory notebook is different from the historical journal. In a memory notebook, you can keep a running list of memories that you wish to write about in more detail in your journal. When you remember something, just record a single sentence, phrase, or date—anything that will remind you of the memory when you decide to write about it. Use each page in your notebook to record a single event. Remember, keep your notes short. This is not the time to write about the whole event. That's what your journal is for.

Mining the Mother Lode

Each day when you begin to write in your historical journal, have your memory notebook by your side. Turn to the first page and read the notes you've written. Close your eyes.

Bring that event to mind and picture it as it happened. Allow yourself to feel the emotions you experienced at that time, imagine what the temperature was, try to recall what you were wearing, and so on. Then, when it is once again fresh in your mind, write about it.

When you have finished writing about that memory, put a big check mark on the page in your notebook so you know you've already told that story in your journal. As you continue to make those check marks on page after page of your memory notebook, you'll feel a great sense of accomplishment.

If you fill up your memory notebook quickly, don't feel that you have too many things to write about. Think of it as a rich mine from which you must extract the resources. Just address one story at a time. Check off each story and move on to the next.

Keep Those Fingers Moving

Whether you record your memories with pen and paper or by typing them into a computer, the important thing is to keep the memories coming and the fingers moving. Don't let anything distract you during your scheduled writing time.

You may choose to write about one event each day and write it as completely as you can remember, or you may want to write two or more shorter entries. Many of the people I've spoken with end up writing about more than one memory each day because they have so much fun. Your journal becomes very much like a child sitting beside you just waiting to hear the next story.

From One-Liners to Books

How long you make your entry depends entirely upon you. The amount of detail, your style of writing, and the complexity of the event all determine the length of each entry.

It's up to you whether you keep your recollections short and to the point or detailed and as long as a chapter in a book. Try it both ways to see which you like better.

The Whole Story

With a longer entry, you have room to paint a more complete picture of what happened. You can include details that you wouldn't have room to include in a shorter version. You can take time to include dialogue and rich descriptions.

Because of its length, you may decide, as many journal keepers do, to write the entry over several days or weeks. Keep in mind that no one is pushing you to finish. You have no deadlines. You have the luxury of time, so use it. Use as much time to tell the story as you want.

Good Things Come in Small Packages

Sometimes less truly *is* more, and if you opt to write shorter snippets, you will necessarily include less detail and write about an event for only a day or two. If the shorter style suits your personality, then by all means, keep it short!

And don't think that, if you keep shorter entries, they are somehow inferior to longer, more detailed entries. They're just a different style. After a little practice, you'll get quite proficient at cutting to the heart of a story, including the pertinent facts, and reaching the end in a very short entry. That, in itself, is a great skill.

The Write Idea

Although you'll be recording your memory the way you remember it, you may find that someone else remembers it differently. That's just a fact of life. As Pablo Picasso said, "If there were only one truth, you couldn't paint a hundred canvases on the same theme."

Words of Wisdom

"Life is too short for a long story."

—Lady Mary Wortley Montagu

We're Not Writing on Stone Here

If you start out with longer entries and decide you'd prefer to switch to shorter snippets, you can always make the change. Don't feel that, because you start out one way, you have to continue in that manner to the end.

The beauty of a journal is that you make the rules. You set the guidelines, and you can change them at any time to suit your needs. It never works the other way around. The journal never dictates to you.

Put Your Best Foot Forward

However you choose to write your historical journal, always take care to write in your very best style and keep in mind the great-grandchild or historian who might read your words someday. What do you want them to know about your life and times? What can you teach them about your time and place with your entry?

In fact, you may encounter some memories with very important lessons to teach. In those cases, record the memory and then address a short note to whoever might be reading it in times to come. Teach the lesson. Tell them exactly what you'd say if they were sitting beside you listening to your story. You never know who will benefit from your words.

Words of Wisdom

"It's a pleasure to share one's memories. Everything remembered is dear, endearing, touching, precious. At least the past is safe—though we didn't know it at the time. We know it now. Because it's in the past; because we have survived."

—Susan Sontag

Take the time to consider and write about the things closest to your heart and at the forefront of your memory. Keep your writing fresh and lively, and it will take your memory into the future.

Family Memories

In addition to first-person accounts, you can record family stories in your historical journal. Think of all the anecdotes you heard as a child about your parents, grandparents, or your favorite Aunt Maude.

No one probably took the time to record these stories before, but you can do it now. They might be a little fuzzy, but write what you can remember.

If you share your journal entries with family members and friends, they might be able to help you fill in the blanks and even suggest new memories to record. By all means, tap into others' memories if they are available. Ask them questions and come away with a wealth of information.

At Your Grandfather's Knee

We probably all have fond childhood memories of family members—our parents, aunts and uncles, and grandparents—sitting around the dinner table during family gatherings, sharing memories from the past.

If you're anything like me, you wish you had written down every one of those memories as you heard them. Better yet, I wish relatives had had the foresight to record their own memoirs. But at least I can record the memory fragments I have from those evenings around the kitchen table in long ago childhood days, and so can you in your own historical journal.

Think back to a time in childhood when you sat with an older relative as he or she related a childhood story. Describe that memory in your historical journal as well as you can remember it. After you've recorded the memory, take a few minutes to explain how old you were when you heard it, who told it to you, and why it is special.

Ask and Ask Again

You have another source for family memories: your relatives. People love to talk about themselves, but they often decline for fear of getting too carried away. However, if you ask them to tell you everything they remember about special family times, family weddings, or some other topic, they will gladly begin to tell you all they know.

Of course, some relatives will tell you more stories than others, but don't feel you have to include everything in your journal. Choose only those that reveal a certain characteristic about a person or a particularly funny or poignant story. This is, after all, your journal. Use your relatives' recollections to enrich and enhance your own journal, but don't let them take command.

We Gather Together

If you don't see your relatives very often, you may have the opportunity to ask them about their memories at family gatherings such as family reunions, holidays, and special occasions. At times like these, people generally are in a wonderful mood and willing to share their memories.

Take advantage of every situation you can to learn more about your family and, indeed, yourself. I'm sure your aunts and uncles can tell you stories about yourself when you were a baby, like the time you swallowed a dime or when you made a funny remark at the dinner table. Don't be afraid to ask; that's the only way you're going to learn.

Putting Pen to Paper

Ninety percent of all the entries in your historical journal should revolve around you. The other 10 percent can be stories about other people and things. After all, this *is your* historical journal!

Particular Memories to Include

Now that you have all these recollections and you've started to list them in your memory notebook, you have to decide which to include in your historical journal. In the rest of this chapter, I'll suggest some things you can focus on in your journal that will make writing interesting for you and reading interesting for someone in the future.

The Write Idea

Disasters tend to bring out the best and the worst in people. After a tornado decimates a town, you may find someone trying to sell water for $10 a gallon while someone else donates a huge truckload of the same commodity. By writing about your disaster experiences, you can capture the real essence of people—their true character. At the same time, you'll be writing your own adventure story that future generations will relish.

➤ **Siblings.** Consider writing about special moments you shared with a brother or sister. If you grew apart over time, write about that. Were you particularly close to one sibling and not another? Explore why. Did you and your brother or sister have favorite games or projects? Tell it all to your journal!

➤ **Precious moments.** We can all remember at least a few moments each week that were particularly special to us. Perhaps a co-worker's pat on the back made a difference in your day. Maybe a child saying "I love you" helped you put things in perspective. Think back on those special moments and write about them in your journal.

➤ **Disasters.** Floods, earthquakes, hurricanes, tornadoes, mudslides … the list of natural disasters can fill a page. If you survived a tornado, were evacuated from a flood, or were rattled by an earthquake, by all means write about these things in your journal.

Words of Wisdom

"Teachers open the door, but you must enter by yourself."

—Chinese proverb

➤ **World events.** Where were you when you heard that JFK had been shot? Or that the Berlin Wall had been torn down? Haven't we all been asked these kinds of questions? World events will be recorded in history books and studied for hundreds of years, and you can provide your own perspective on them by recording your experiences in your historical journal.

➤ **Teachers.** Think where you would be without teachers in your life. They taught you everything from the basics of everyday living to the intricacies of calculus. We owe them much more than we can ever repay. Remember them in your journal as the exceptional people they are.

➤ **The wisdom of books.** Write about what you read. The knowledge could be as simple as the fact that King Henry VIII of England had six wives. You may not have known that before, and how marvelous for you that you know it now. If you fill your journal with all these little things and what they mean to you, your entire journal will become a font of knowledge that you never dreamed you could write.

➤ **Life's lessons.** No formal education can duplicate the real-life experiences we gain from the "school of hard knocks." I know we've all attended this auspicious institution of learning, and the lessons we came away with were hard-won and long-remembered. Use your journal as the perfect place to record these experiences and reflect on them. Try to figure out how you can use this new knowledge in the future and prevent similar mistakes.

Words of Wisdom

"Each man must look to himself to teach him the meaning of life. It is not something discovered; it is something molded."

—Antoine de Saint-Exupéry

Just Like Old Photographs

Whenever we see old black-and-white photographs or sepia tone prints, we have to remind ourselves that the world looked very different from the picture we hold in our hand. Vibrant reds and brilliant yellows colored the world in the same way they do today. The sun shone as brightly, and the sky was just as blue.

The memories you record in your historical journal will remind you and those who come after you that your life in years past had every bit of the vitality it does today or will tomorrow. Time and distance may have conferred upon you a kind of safety in your reminiscence, but they have not drained your memories of life or color.

Once more, breathe life into times past with your journal. Relive the good and the bad. Don't be afraid of the emotions. Embrace them. Remember loved ones, events, and lessons learned and then use those lessons to live tomorrow well.

The Least You Need to Know

➤ An historical journal emphasizes past events rather than present moments.

➤ Family members can serve as valuable sources of memories for you to record.

➤ A collection of your memories can serve as your informal autobiography.

➤ You can acknowledge in your historical journal all the people and events that have influenced your life.

Chapter 16

Other Types of Journals

In This Chapter

➤ Hitting the road with your journal

➤ Putting your hobby on paper

➤ The writer's journal

➤ The best-known secret formula

In addition to the types of journals I've already discussed in this book, myriad others exist, each serving a particular purpose. I'd like to close this section, however, with a brief discussion of three other journals: travel logs, hobby diaries, and writer's journals. I hope these descriptions will give you enough information to develop any additional journals you feel will fulfill your specific needs.

Remember that your journal is your outlet for self-expression, a means to take control, a vehicle to safeguard your memories, and a place to plan your future. Embrace this very valuable tool. Mold it and shape it to your needs, and it will serve you well.

The Travel Log

We sometimes refer to vacations as the opportunity to "get away from it all." And indeed, we need to do just that from time to time. Unplugging and leaving the cares of everyday life behind has a way of recharging our batteries. But when you do get away, don't leave your journal behind, particularly if this is the vacation you have dreamed of and planned for years.

Take your journal with you as a companion to tell all the things you've seen and all the wonderful things you've done. You'll meet people along the way and will want to write about your impressions of them. Record anything you find remarkable. It'll make interesting reading in years to come.

Words of Wisdom

"To get away from one's working environment is, in a sense, to get away from one's self; and this is often the chief advantage of travel and change."

—Charles Horton Cooley, *Human Nature and the Social Order*

How Much Did You Say?

People often think of travel journals as a record of gas mileage and prices, hotel costs, meals, and other expenses. It depends on your personality how detailed you'd like to get with all of this, but many people like the idea. You may be one of them.

If you decide to record all the details about expenses, miles traveled, and directions taken, then at the end of the trip, you can add up miles and expenses and quantify the vacation. For instance, you'll be able to tell people that, in a two-week period, you traveled 3,542 miles, spent $1,216 on hotels, $1,797 on meals, and $723 on gas. Now that's impressive. Besides, in years to come, it might be fun to go back and compare prices.

If This Is Tuesday ...

While you keep track of miles and dollars and cents, don't forget to record other aspects of your trip. If you're vacationing right, you'll forget about what day it is as well as what's happening in the rest of the world. The only news you'll hear are little snippets on the radio as you travel or a quick headline on TV. Don't feel guilty. That's exactly what you need to do on vacation.

While you leave the rest of the world behind, you immerse yourself in a whole new environment: the mountains, the beach, the desert, the city, or wherever you've chosen to spend your time. If you take a moment, I'll bet you'll notice that you breathe easier and step lighter. You smile more easily and truly begin to relax.

At the end of each day, write about your experiences in your diary. Tell where you went. Describe what you did. Talk about all the fun you had. Do you feel more relaxed? Do you feel a little happier? Is your mind a bit more peaceful? Acknowledgment of these positive changes in yourself will help you better appreciate them.

Change of Scenery

One of the reasons we leave home and go on vacation is for a change of scenery. Somehow new environs have a way of putting us in a better frame of mind.

Whatever the reason, accept it. See as many new things and open yourself to as many new experiences as you can.

Allow yourself to marvel at new sights. Give yourself permission to laugh openly when you encounter something humorous. And don't forget to stop now and then in your frantic itinerary to watch a sunset. Write about all of these things in your journal. You don't want to forget about the beauty of the caverns you toured or the fine art in the museum. And you certainly want to remember the way they made you feel.

People Matter

Just as you write about where you went and what you did on your vacation, include comments about the people you met. You may meet someone and immediately recognize that you share something in common. You know you'll never see the person again, yet the encounter touches you in some way.

By all means, write about these people in your journal. Describe them and your time together, however brief. Then, of course, don't forget to mention what made them so memorable.

A Second Vacation

When you get back home and start living your regular life again, you can relive your trip and feel a little bit like you're on vacation again by rereading your journal.

A Hobby Journal

We each have something that captures our imagination. Some may find fascination in the stars, others in the sea. Millions love to tend their gardens or create tiny worlds within the confines of a model railroad platform. All these hobbies pass the time, occupy the mind, and nurture the soul. Yes, believe it or not, hobbies cultivate the spirit because they encourage play, which turns into exploration.

If you already have a hobby, you know how it satisfies something deep inside.

Putting Pen to Paper

Consider leaving blank spaces in your journal as you write so you can add photographs of places you visit and people you meet. Don't worry about getting the photos developed while you're on vacation. If you wait until you get back home, you can extend your vacation by adding the photos then.

Putting Pen to Paper

It seems like, on every trip, we meet someone with whom we have nothing in common, while for some reason they take an immediate liking to us. Don't forget to write about these people in your journal, too. In their own way, they are worth remembering.

Getting Started

If you don't already enjoy a hobby, I encourage you to find one. Explore possibilities and write about them in your journal. Talk about what gives you pleasure and how you'd like to spend your free time. Once you find a hobby that you enjoy, write about it in your journal.

If you already spend time at a hobby, whether it is gardening or metalworking, then keep a record of your projects: What gave you the idea? How did you prepare for it? What steps did you take along the way to completion? What enjoyment did you take from it afterward?

Words of Wisdom

"God Almighty first planted a garden. And indeed, it is the purest of human pleasures."

—Francis Bacon

The Write Idea

Millions of people enjoy a host of hobbies and recreational activities every year. For example, the Boat Owners Association of the United States has a membership of 500,000; Family Campers and Rivers, 56,000 families; and the National Model Railroad Association, 25,000 people.

Hobbies allow us to express ourselves in so many ways. How nice to keep a hobby journal as a record.

The Writer's Journal

Writers are always writing, whether on paper, on keyboards, or in their minds. Ideas surface. They consider new ways of tackling a subject for an article or formulating a whole story. As writers, we embrace the freedom of expression we enjoy in this country to tell stories, voice opinions, create images, describe the past, and look to the future. You may have an unpopular view on an issue that you wish to express, or may have a new idea. Sometimes the ideas overwhelm us, however, and we can't always satisfy the urge to write about them. Sometimes the opposite happens, and we experience that dreaded thing called writer's block. In either case, a writer's journal can help you out.

The Writer's Mindset

Writers know that, in order to publish articles and books, they have to come up with fresh and different ideas to interest readers and publishers. They recognize that everything they do, everywhere they go, and every person they meet might become the subject for their next article or book. You can record any experience or encounter that might be useful in your writing in your writer's journal.

A Dime a Dozen

Ideas may be a dime a dozen, but *great* ideas are few and far between, and you can never tell which is which without a little bit of exploration and thought.

Your journal is the perfect place to explore ideas to determine whether or not to pursue them. Let me show you how it works for magazine articles.

Once you get an idea, write it down in your journal. Then develop a short outline on the subject. In a few short sentences and phrases, you can outline an entire article.

Keep your outline simple and short. You'll be able to return to it and flesh it out whenever you're ready to write about it.

Embrace Technology

If you decide to keep a writer's journal, you may find it easier to keep it on computer than in a book. A computer can save you a great deal of time and trouble and can free you up for the more important task of creating.

You can save a variety of files such as characters, ideas, starts, lines, and descriptions. Then, if you want to find a particular line or idea that you wrote about in your journal, you can run a search for it, and in a matter of seconds you'll be able to find it. Once you've found what you are looking for, you can—voilà!—cut and paste it into another document without retyping.

The Write Idea

You don't have to be a published author to keep a writer's journal. If you sit down to put words on paper, you are a writer, particularly if you do it with publication in mind. As a writer, ideas for stories, characters, even lines of dialogue come to you all the time. A writer's journal will help you manage them and store them for future use.

Great Lines

As a writer, snippets of conversation, description, and narrative always manage to invade my thoughts. I don't know where they come from or where they're going. I have no idea what characters or story they pertain to, but they're marvelous bits of dialogue. I'm sure that, if you're a writer, the same thing happens to you. When it does, don't ignore these wonderful words. Record them in your journal.

You might try to organize them as you write them. For instance, suppose you thought of a line like, "She walked with the assurance of a stalking lioness." Create a heading called "Walked like ..." and place it in that category. When you need to describe how someone walked, you can look through your file and choose the most appropriate image.

Great Starts

Have you ever had an idea for a project while in the middle of another? Of course you have, but you have to finish the project at hand before you start on the next. Yet the new idea keeps nagging at your brain. You may even have the whole first section of it whirling around in your head.

Don't jump into the new project with both feet, but do take a few minutes to write it down in your journal.

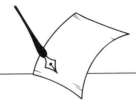

Putting Pen to Paper

When writer's block occurs, your journal is an ideal tool to get those creative juices flowing again. You can write about your lack of ideas or motivation, and you can try out new ideas for an article or chapter. When you suffer from writer's block, the most important thing to do is to keep writing, and your writer's journal is the perfect place to do just that! Of course, what you've written doesn't have to have anything to do with your assignment or current project. What matters is that you wrote something. Sometimes, if you just get your hand moving, the words and ideas you need will come.

Great Characters

Writing fiction is heady stuff because, after all, you create situations, societies, and people, and then you set about manipulating them all to serve the purposes of your plot. You fashion an entire little world.

Of all the elements of a novel you may create, characters are by far the most complex. One way to create memorable characters is to make a character sketch. This is where you write down all the physical, mental, and behavioral traits of your character as well as his or her background and history.

In all likelihood, you won't be able to develop a character at a single sitting, so take your time. Write about the person in your journal as if he or she was your best friend and you knew everything about him or her. Let's face it. You do. You created the person. Who better to write about him or her? But be careful to create characters for very specific plots. In time, you may come to think of your journal as a nursery.

Let Your Imagination Roam

However you make a living or spend your leisure time, you can make use of a journal. You have many to choose from as well as the ability to mix and match to create a unique hybrid. Find the time. Make the time. Do whatever you have to do to take advantage of this powerful tool.

We all have so much that we hold in our hearts; we have so many memories that we wish to keep close. Don't trust it all to memory. Write. Record. Recollect. Let your journal remember it for you.

Use your journal as a sounding board and a way to fire your imagination. Utilize it as a means to grow physically, mentally, and spiritually. Reflect on your life and learn from your experiences. Pay tribute to those who have helped you and take the time to laugh at yourself and the ironies of life.

The beauty of all this is that you will have a running account of your existence. When your grandchildren and great-grandchildren decide to research their family history, you will stand out from the rest of their ancestors. You will become more than a name and a date on the family tree. They will come to know you for the living, breathing, vibrant person you are now because you have taken the time to introduce yourself to them through your journal.

The Least You Need to Know

➤ You can remember the details of a journey or vacation with a travel journal.

➤ Record not only the places you go but also the people you meet to bring your diary alive.

➤ A hobby journal can help you to track your progress and knowledge as well as record your enjoyment of a particular pastime.

➤ Keeping a writer's journal can assist you in managing your ideas or overcoming writer's block.

Part 3

What to Write, What to Write

The variety of journals discussed in the preceding part pales in comparison to the ways in which people use them. Journal keepers have the most wonderful imaginations when it comes to utilizing their diaries and what they deem appropriate subject matter. Their love for journaling has led them to develop their own types of journals, mostly hybrids of existing kinds, and they constantly surprise me with stories of what they've chosen to include in their journals.

They write about special occasions and everyday events. They include the mundane and the stellar. Some keep a single journal, while others keep several at a time. In their journal, they have found a friend, a refuge, and a safe haven for their memories. In this part, I share with you what I've learned from other journalers as well as from my own years of journaling.

Chapter 17

Special Occasions

In This Chapter

➤ Welcoming the new arrival

➤ A birthday to remember

➤ As the married years pass by

➤ Moving on from graduation

➤ Special wedding memories

➤ Other special occasions to record in your journal

Every New Year's Eve, we bid good-bye to the old year and say an anticipatory hello to the new. We look forward to celebrating birthdays, anniversaries, and a host of special occasions and happy times in the months to come.

Each event brings with it particular emotions and memories of past times. Some of these memories bring a smile; others cause us to shed a tear in bittersweet reminiscence. Use your journal to record all these times to keep them close to your heart and to offer them to the future as a reminder of what once was.

New Beginnings

When we (or someone close to us) give birth, we welcome the new arrival into the family with celebrations and congratulations. A description of the celebration would make a memorable journal entry.

If you are a parent of a new baby, you should take the opportunity to write about these very special days of your child's new life. Write about your emotions. Describe your euphoria. Capture your elation. If you have doubts about your abilities as a parent—and most people do, particularly first-time parents—write about those, too. Once you recognize your doubts and fears and put them on paper, you have more control of the situation, a sentiment that will nurture confidence to do something positive to make those doubts disappear.

You might also see this opportunity as the perfect time to make some promises to yourself and your child.

Words of Wisdom

"You may give them your love
    but not your thoughts.
For they have their own
    thoughts.
You may house their bodies but
    not their souls,
For their souls dwell in the house
    of tomorrow, which you can
    not visit, not even in your
    dreams."

—Kahlil Gibran

Hopes and Dreams

Every parent has hopes and dreams for his or her child. Write about the things you have in your heart. Talk about your wish that this child grow into a good, happy, and healthy person. Write about your wish that he or she finds a mission in life and finds fulfillment. Think how your words will thrill your children when they read about themselves in your journal in years to come.

You might even choose to deal with these issues in the form of an unsent letter. Address the entry to your child personally and write from the heart. Of course you hope you'll have many years together to teach, to love, and to express what you feel, but any parent will tell you that children grow up too quickly. You will never again have the chance to relive these moments. Do it now.

The Write Idea

Children love to read about themselves. You could make the reading of your journal entry from the day of their birth a part of their birthday celebration each year.

To know that you loved them from the beginning and that you had high hopes for them will give your children a feeling of worth that will grow into a deep sense of self. To read about your doubts will present you as a much more approachable person. Both of these factors can serve to strengthen the biological bond you share and enhance it with a far more meaningful, emotional bond.

Paint a Portrait

In addition to your feelings, write about your baby. While totally dependent on you for everything, this child is nevertheless a real and complete person with wants and desires and personality. Seize the chance you've been given and write about these things now. I promise, if you wait too long, you will forget all the wonderful little details.

Begin by describing your child's physical and emotional characteristics. You should find these easy enough considering you started counting fingers and toes the moment you laid eyes on your little bundle of joy. Here are a few questions to get you started:

➤ What color hair does the baby have?

➤ Does the hair on the nape of her neck curl in an endearing way? Or does she have a kind of fine down instead of hair?

➤ Is he robust and healthy?

➤ Is she petite and delicate?

➤ Whom does the child resemble? You? Your spouse? Grandparents? Other relatives?

➤ Does he like to sleep?

➤ Does she have a hearty appetite?

➤ Is he a fussy eater?

➤ Does she smile easily?

➤ Does he love to be cuddled? Rocked?

➤ Does she like to play?

➤ How alert is he?

Remember that these are all impressions you form in the first few days of a child's birth. Take the time to notice what they look like and how they react to the world around them. How interesting it would be in years to come to go back and read these first impressions to see just how accurate you were or if your child has changed.

Continue to consider similar questions on a regular basis as your child grows to track his or her development. Of course, your questions will change as your child matures, but I think you'll find it interesting to note any changes. In fact, recognizing these changes will help you interact with your child more effectively.

The Write Idea

The jury is still out on whether genetics or environment plays a larger role in the development of our personality. Your journal could act as an informal experiment on your part to see just how much of a clue your newborn's behavior gives you in the first few days of life.

Happy Birthday to Me

Birthdays are special times for almost everyone. Whether we are 7, 17, or 70 years old, a birthday is a time to reflect on the year gone by and to think about the past and future. Can you imagine what a wonderful record you would have if you kept a special birthday journal in which you recorded an entry once a year on that special day?

For children, recording in a birthday journal could be a special treat to look forward to every year—a chance to describe the gifts they received and any special memories they have of the year gone by. Teens could write about their plans for the future, and adults can determine whether they are where they thought they would be in their professional and personal lives.

Putting Pen to Paper

Consider giving a birthday journal to a child or teen as a birthday gift. You can write the first entry in the journal, telling the child how you feel about him and encouraging him to record in his journal every year on his birthday.

It Doesn't Seem Like Twenty-Five Years

Every time our wedding anniversary comes around, my husband tells me, "It doesn't seem like that many years." When I ask him exactly how many years it seems like, he backs off and says something clever like, "However many years it seems like, they've all been wonderful." You can't argue with that logic.

The fact remains that time does seem to pass quickly, and before you know it, you're celebrating another year gone by. Think about the deeply held secrets you could write in your journal on these days.

The Good Ones and the Not-So-Good Ones

Whether you've been happily married for several years or are struggling to keep a marriage together, you have a lot to write about, and an anniversary is a good time to take the opportunity to do so.

Write about experiences in the past year that have helped or hurt your marriage. Tell how your love has changed over the years. If you have children, relate how they have affected your lives and how they affect you now. Describe how you have supported each other in various situations.

Give examples of the little things you've done for each other to express your love. Are there any particularly funny situations that stand out from the past year? How about poignant moments? If you haven't already recorded them, include them now.

If your marriage is on the rocks, perhaps a reflective journal, as discussed in Chapter 11, can help you figure out what went wrong and can be used as a tool to help repair your relationship. Treat your journal as a sounding board and learn what you can to improve future relationships.

Life After School

Graduation is an important time in our lives. It marks the end of an era and the beginning of a new adventure in life. Whether you're graduating from high school or college, take the time to record what you're feeling in your journal.

After High School

If you will soon be graduating from high school, take the time to write about your plans, hopes, and dreams in your journal. Write about your excitement about attending college or what you look forward to in the service. Perhaps you see advancement and success in the job you've landed.

If you have no immediate plans, write about that, too. It could be a good time to think clearly about what you'd really like to do with your future. This is a once-in-a-lifetime opportunity. Don't let it pass by without some sort of heartfelt record.

After College

Believe it or not, there is life after college. The years of classes, tests, papers, dorm life, friends, and late-night pizzas eventually come to an end. The prospect of graduation is daunting because now everyone will expect you to go out into the world with diploma in hand and find a great way to make a living. You also realize that a whole way of life is ending, never to be revisited.

Thus, you may face college graduation with some ambivalence. Use that ambivalence to your advantage. Write about it in your journal. You might even write about your idea of the perfect future. Seeing it on paper may prompt you to begin a whole new type of journal, a log as described in Chapter 6, to help you achieve that wonderful future you envision for yourself.

Explore the possibilities. Describe your ideal job. Would it be an indoor job or an outdoor one? Would you interact with many people or work alone? Would you do research? Become involved in technology? Perhaps sales? Think seriously about what has the most appeal to you and then use your log journal to set goals and make your plan for achievement.

Special Wedding Memories

Of course, you can't forget about weddings. They bring about one of the most profound changes in your life—the commitment of sharing your life with another person. You can use your journal to write about your wedding plans, to describe how you are feeling, and to record the details of the big day.

A day or two after your honeymoon, when you have a moment to yourself, take out your journal and write about all the things that went through your mind at the moment you said, "I do." That had to have been an exceptional moment for you; you don't want to depend on your memory to keep a complete record. Your journal can perform that service for you beautifully.

The Write Idea

Keeping a theme journal, as described in Chapter 10, for your wedding plans will help you cope with the stress leading up to the big day.

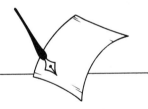

Putting Pen to Paper

You can also use your wedding journal to write about your new family—the in-laws—and the home you share with your new spouse.

Other Special Events

The other special occasions in our life vary from person to person and culture to culture. You will have your own set of special occasions that you will want to write about.

I discussed a few suggestions for you in this section, but I'm sure your creativity will lead you to many more. Remember that it's not so much the event itself that has significance for you; it's the effect that it has on you.

Religious Events

Religion plays a central role for some people, and each faith has its own set of rituals to mark particular points in a person's spiritual journey. Often, months of preparation and study are involved before the actual ceremony. During this time, the person may be involved in a great deal of soul searching, and this is the perfect time for a spiritual journal, much like the one described in Chapter 12.

When the special day arrives, whatever feelings you experience as you take part in the ritual are wonderful material for your journal. Think what great lessons you could teach to generations that follow you. How did the ceremony touch you? What did you think about? Were you inspired in any way? How will this change your life? You should address all these questions and more to make your journal entry complete for this day.

Awards and Recognition

When others recognize the excellence of your actions with an award, it gives you a feeling of accomplishment and appreciation. For most people, these times happen few and far between in a lifetime, and you should definitely record them.

Write about the circumstances leading up to the award and how you found out about it. Was it a surprise? Did someone tell you about it ahead of time? Did you have to prepare an acceptance speech? What did the recognition entail? A certificate? A plaque? A cash prize? Something named in your honor?

Whatever the situation, I'm sure everything surrounding the event would be most memorable and something you'll always want to remember. Think of your great-grandchildren and how proud they will be when they read about the wonderful things you've done.

Ordinary People with Special Lives

Most of us lead pretty normal lives from day to day with the occasional punctuation of very special events. They add the spice, the encouragement, and an escape from the ordinary. They provide entertainment, camaraderie, and a reason for self-examination and reflection.

Ordinary life becomes not so ordinary, and these events allow us to put the everyday behind us for a while. They open the door a bit for a very extraordinary part of us to come out and shine. Take this glow and put it down on paper in such a way that you will remember it always and others will appreciate it.

The Least You Need to Know

➤ Special occasions add an extra dimension to our life and deserve to be recorded.

➤ When writing about special times, be sure to include the good experiences as well as the bad experiences.

➤ Recording special events gives you a unique opportunity to address the overwhelming emotions you may be feeling at these times.

Chapter 18

Life's Little Pleasures

In This Chapter

➤ Appreciating life's little pleasures

➤ Appreciating the beauty of the natural world

➤ Letting the arts touch us

➤ The funnies of life

Life is not boring. Face it, we never know what's waiting around the corner to surprise us. It could be as simple as a delicious, toasted ham-and-cheese sandwich or as important as someone declaring their love for us. The fact that we never know what our future holds makes life all that much sweeter. Now, if we did know everything ahead of time, that would be boring, wouldn't it?

Take the time to smell the roses and write about the sweet fragrance. Give yourself permission to open your mind and your heart to the wonderful things around you. Let the experience suffuse you and then write about every little detail of it. Indeed, think how rich and full your life could be if you found the joy everywhere and in everyone and held on to it forever.

Your journal can help you do just that. Once you write it down, you can revisit the delight of the moment and once more warm your heart whenever you have the need.

Kids Say the Darndest Things

Children have a certain innocence about them, particularly the very young. As they take on the task of learning all they need to know to get through life, their brain constantly takes in all manner of information and makes all sorts of connections.

Take the time to watch and listen to the children in your life. Not only will they give you joy, their innocence may spark an idea or give you some insight into a deeper question.

What Did You Say?

As the mother of three children, I could go on and on about some of the funny things my children have said and done, but I'll spare you and share just one story.

In 1984, my husband came home with our very first computer, an IBM PCjr with 256KB of memory. It created quite a stir in our household with our daughters, then seven and nine years old. After my husband set up the machine and patiently answered all our questions, we sat down to dinner, and the discussion naturally centered around the new computer. Somehow the conversation took a different direction, and we started talking about guardian angels.

Our nine-year-old said, "I'll bet they follow you around, taking notes in a little notebook and keeping track of all the good things and bad things you do."

Our seven-year-old promptly corrected her, saying, "Oh, no. Everything's on disk these days."

You can bet that's a solid-gold journal entry.

You, too, will encounter comments like this from the children in your life. Make note of them. Remember them and keep them close to your heart. Your entries will make it possible for you to look back in time, relive those special moments with a smile, and remind you all over again how much you love your children.

Putting Pen to Paper

Aside from all the things around you that give you joy, look to the people in your life. We laugh and we cry with these special people. They make an everyday lunch memorable. Go to your journal and write about these extraordinary people and the times you share.

Out of the Rut

As you go about your day-to-day business, avoid the temptation to put yourself on automatic pilot. Take a moment here and a moment there to look around you. Observe the clouds floating by. Watch the wind rustle in the trees and remember a time, a feeling, a thought that you associate with things from your past.

Allow yourself the time to smile at a stranger, and at the same time, let someone do something nice for you. These little delights add up to the larger joy of living, they improve your quality of life, and heighten the interest level of your journal.

Kindnesses

Nothing elicits a smile more surely than a random act of kindness. Whether you are the recipient or perpetrator, thoughtfulness brings a little unexpected pleasure to life and feeds the soul. If you keep a reflective or spiritual journal, pay particular attention to these little moments and how they affect you.

Give a little. Get a little. Take note of the feelings of warmth that suffuse you. Get in touch with your spirit and write about the growing awareness of that unseen part of you.

The Roses

Nature offers us opportunities every day to find pleasure in life. Sunrises and sunsets offer perfect examples of common occurrences of uncommon beauty, particularly if you share the experience with a loved one.

Enjoy the sight of a bird or the graceful flight of a deer. Lie down under a shade tree and feel the breeze dance across your face. Note the blue of the sky or the brightness of a flower. Feel the delight in your soul and then share the wonderful feelings with your journal.

You don't have to live in the country to experience these natural wonders. The city offers its own natural splendors. Watch the sailboats on the town lake or the wildlife along the shores of the river. Take note of the rain on the pavement and the whistle of the wind through the flagpole. Nature is all around us everywhere we go. Slow down enough to notice it. Let it remind you of your bond with everything around you and then go write about it.

Open Your Mind

The little pleasures of life abound; we need only open our mind to them. Art, music, poetry, and humor all offer us a wealth of ways to enrich our life. Not everyone will find himself or herself drawn to the same things. You might find a Picasso enthralling; the person next to you might find it incomprehensible. Your friend may laugh raucously at a joke while you stare in bewilderment.

We live among a veritable treasure trove of art. It's available everywhere, from a discount market to the Internet. We must only open our eyes to find it and open our mind to feed our spirit.

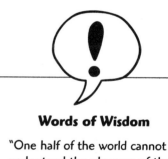

Words of Wisdom

"One half of the world cannot understand the pleasures of the other."

—Jane Austen

The Sound of Music

You can find any type of music in a music store, on the radio, or on the Internet. Whether you relate best to classical music, rock 'n' roll, jazz, the blues, or hip hop, fill your life with music and let it speak to you. What does it say? What do you think

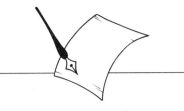

about when you hear it? Music can provoke some very interesting questions and answers. It can evoke feelings and dredge up memories. Listen for them and record them in your journal. They're too precious to forget.

The Rhyme and Reason

For many people, poetry touches them in ways that no other form of writing can. If you're one of those people, write about the poems that are meaningful to you in your journal. If you are inspired to, write your own.

You can use poetry in your journal as a means to explore certain aspects of your personality. If a certain poem touches you, write about it and why you think it has particular significance to you. Sometimes an event, a person, or a feeling is so overwhelming, a poem might gush forth. Write it in your journal as a permanent record of what you're feeling at this moment.

Putting Pen to Paper

If you find that you are moved by a particular piece of music, be sure to get the name of the song and record it in your journal. Then describe why it touched you. If you do this often enough, you might be able to recognize a pattern in your tastes and thus learn something new about yourself.

I Know What I Like

You don't have to stop at poetry in your journal. Let yourself be visually creative as well. Draw on the pages of your journal. You could render a diagram of a new machine you have in mind or the design of a dress you'd like. Don't talk about it. Don't describe it. Show it in a drawing. Perhaps you saw a bird outside your window today and it captured your imagination. Draw that bird and tell how you felt.

Never let any doubts about your talent keep you from writing or drawing. After all, not many of us have paintings hanging in galleries, but we all have some talent for art, however small. Wouldn't you appreciate a sketch of your grandmother's dream house done by her own hand? How about a sketch of next spring's garden rendered by your grandfather? Of course you would.

Simple line drawings could make a point. Stick figures could show some action. Don't limit yourself to words. Let the muse take control of your hand and draw like you have never drawn before. You may discover some latent talent, but no matter what, you'll have fun!

Humor

They say that laughter is the best medicine. Whether or not laughter really does have the power to heal, there's no question that it is one of the great pleasures of life. Don't be afraid to laugh. So what if little laugh lines form around your mouth. You'll have a lot of fun putting them there! And when you write about the things that make you laugh, I guarantee that they will give you cause to smile again. Besides, tomorrow may not be as much fun. You can always go back and relive the happy moment.

"Good Grief, Charlie Brown!"

Whenever I pick up the morning paper, I first reach for the comics. Forget the headlines. Forget the stock market. Forget sports. I want to laugh first thing in the morning. Every once in a while, I'll read a cartoon that makes me laugh extra hard or one that rings true. I have no choice but to cut it out and keep it forever. Guess where I put it? Yep, my journal!

If you enjoy the comics, why don't you do the same? Cut one out and add it to your journal entry for the day. Glue it onto your journal page and write why you think it's so funny or so apropos.

The Write Idea

Norman Cousins wrote extensively about the healing power of laughter in his best-selling book, *The Healing Heart.*

Go Ahead, Make Me Laugh!

"Why did the chicken cross the road?"

"To get to the other side."

As a child, you probably thought this joke enormously funny, but as an adult, you just chuckle at the memory. How could you have thought it was so funny? Now the jokes we laugh at range from the base to the very sophisticated, and some make us laugh more than others.

Words of Wisdom

"You could read Kant by yourself, if you wanted; but you must share a joke with someone else."

—Robert Louis Stevenson

You should let others tell you jokes, even if you've heard them before. You should tell your own, even if you're not very good at it, to which I plead guilty. If you have a favorite joke, write it down in your journal. Should you ever forget it, you will always have a record to go back to.

Nearly every time I go back to reread portions of my journal, I have to laugh again at some old joke someone told me. Not only does it make me laugh again, it brings to mind the person who shared his or her humor with me.

If someone plays a practical joke on you, put it down in your journal. You never know when you may have to use it for your own purposes. If you plan to play a joke on someone, try to predict his or her reaction and then write about what really happened. You can have such fun with this.

The Pleasures

Look for the little pleasures life has to offer on a daily basis. You don't have to have a million dollars to watch a bird construct a nest or to play with a puppy. You can find pleasure everywhere: among the people we love, in nature, in the arts, and in the lighter side of the spirit. Pleasure feeds the soul, something we must do to remain whole and healthy beings.

Wherever you find your pleasure, be sure to seek it out regularly and open yourself to new ones. Use them to explore yourself and others. Draw upon them for new truths and knowledge. Then write what you've learned in your journal because what you've learned is too precious to forget.

The Least You Need to Know

➤ The people in your life can be a source of great joy.

➤ The arts add a dimension to life that we cannot ignore and should record in our journal.

➤ Nature reminds us of our connection with all of life around us.

➤ Writing about humorous experiences will help you remember not only the silliness but also the people you shared it with.

Chapter 19

Life's Reversals

In This Chapter

➤ Saying good-bye for the last time

➤ Losing your job

➤ When the dust settles

➤ Bad relationships

We all know firsthand about life's ups and downs, its pleasures, and its pains. No one makes it through without having to cope with his or her share of annoyances, setbacks, and losses.

We look forward to the happy times and remember them fondly, but the fact remains, we have to deal with the tough times as well. Write about them in your journal, everything from the little annoyances to the tragedies. They all contribute to who we are and how we perceive life, and writing about them can help us cope and keep our perspective.

In this chapter, I'll describe how you can use your journal as a tool to get you through life when it takes a turn for the worse. Along the way, I will suggest particular types of journals that might be most appropriate and will refer you to the chapter that discusses them in detail.

Saying Good-Bye

We try to deal with losses—whether it's the loss of a loved one, a job, or a relationship—in the best way we know how and try to get on with life, but sometimes we need a little help.

Friends and relatives may offer us a great deal of support, emotional and otherwise, but even with the people we hold most dear, we may have thoughts and feelings we choose not to share. Yet we must express them; otherwise, we may fail to move on. Your journal can give you the outlet you need to cope with loss.

The Last Good-Bye

The Spanish influence on our Anglo culture is so great that a great many Spanish words have made their way into our language, among them the beautiful word *adiós*. Loosely translated, it means good-bye, but as in most instances, something gets lost in the translation.

Words of Wisdom

"As virtuous men pass mildly
   away,
And whisper to their souls to go,
Whilst some of their sad
   friends do say,
The breath goes now, and some
   say no."

—John Donne

The Write Idea

The five stages of grief are denial, anger, bargaining, depression, and acceptance.

Adiós means to go with God, and carries with it the meaning of giving the care of the individual over to the Creator. Good-byes are hard enough, but the last good-bye can be devastating.

Dealing with the Final Good-Bye

We each face death of the physical body, the final function of life. No one escapes. When we lose a loved one, we normally experience the various stages of grief. While you must be strong and not fall apart into a thousand pieces, you also have to allow yourself to bend and to mourn.

The first step in dealing with grief is to recognize that the person you loved is gone from your life. It's often difficult to do, but you can use your journal as a means of exploring this idea. You can write about what the person meant to you, about your fears of continuing life without him or her, and about how you wish he or she was still living.

If there were things you wished you had told the person while he or she was still living, read Chapter 9, "The Unsent Letter," to learn how to do so. Many people find a cathartic journal, discussed in Chapter 8, particularly useful to work through grief. It will help you cope and feel so much better.

Once you have accepted the person's death and are ready to move on with your life, you can use a healing journal, discussed in Chapter 7 to help you mend your broken heart and find the joy in life again.

Putting Pen to Paper

If someone you love dies suddenly, leaving you no chance to express your feelings, consider writing one or more unsent letters. It doesn't matter that you're not face to face or that the person will never read what you've written. The important thing is that you say what you need to say so that you can come to grips with your loss and accept it as a fact of life.

When Marriages End in Divorce

Things can get ugly during a divorce, especially when children, property, and money are involved. During the divorce, you'll experience a whole gamut of emotions and stages of grief for this dying relationship. Depending on your personality, you'll want to cry in sorrow, shout in anger, or huddle in a corner somewhere to hide from the world. Go ahead and grieve. Do whatever you need to feel better but then take control.

Consider keeping a cathartic journal to get all of the negative feelings out of your system. You'll probably experience anger, betrayal, and fear all at once, and you can work through all of these emotions in your cathartic journal.

When you and your other half write your names on the dotted line, officially putting an end to your marriage, grab your journal and write. Write about all the feelings rushing through you and about all the things you wish you had done or said.

Putting Pen to Paper

Many people who have recently lost someone close find themselves in need of spiritual guidance. A spiritual journal, discussed in Chapter 12, can be the perfect companion for your spiritual journey.

The Downside of Downsizing

The corporate world has undergone a number of changes in the last 10 to 15 years. Previously, the goal of corporate employees was to find a secure job with good pay and benefits from which they would eventually retire. In the last several years, a vast transformation has taken place.

Downsizing, outsourcing, and new business philosophies have kicked in, changing the face of American industry. People now move from company to company with more frequency than ever before, and by and large, they have no idea what company they will retire from until the time comes.

Identity Crisis

There's no question that losing a job can prove devastating. Granted, the loss of income is a major setback, but the perceived loss of identity is often the real culprit for the emotional upheaval. If this happens to you, as it does to a large portion of the population these days, you can use your journal not only to help you get through the loss but to find a new job.

The Write Idea

Statistically, men more than women define themselves in terms of what they do rather than who they are.

Getting on with It

In the case of a job loss, two different styles of journal could benefit you. Begin with a cathartic journal to work through your anger and resentment. Vent as much as you need to, then switch to a log journal to chart your course and find your way to a brighter future.

On Your Own

If you decide to become an entrepreneur, you are far from being alone. According to a 1998 Department of Labor survey, 11.2 million people work part-time or full-time in a home-based business. Millions of others opt for a location outside the home in the retail, service, or construction industries. Many new businesses fail, but there are some huge success stories.

Words of Wisdom

"Much of our American progress has been the product of the individual who had an idea; pursued it; fashioned it; tenaciously clung to it against all odds; and then produced it, sold it, and profited from it."

—Hubert H. Humphrey

A log journal can help you decide whether this is the right course of action for you and your family. It will help you keep track of your very first forays into becoming self-employed as well as recording your business goals, plans, successes, and failures.

You can keep track of what worked for you and what didn't. You can record contact names, make important notes, and begin putting your business plan together. Your journal can grow from a simple book to get you started on the path of free enterprise into an important asset filled with valuable information.

Back to Work

On the other hand, if you decide you'd rather look for another job in the corporate world, then by all means do so. Only you know what is best for you and your family, but you can use a log journal to help you make your decision.

In your journal, make a list of the companies to which you are considering applying and list the pros and cons for each company or job that attracts your attention. Keep track of all the companies to which you send your resumé as well as your interviews, contact names, dates, and the results of those interviews. One way or another, you can get yourself back into the workforce.

When the Dust Settles

Loss comes with the territory of human existence, and we have to deal with it the best way we can. Family, friends, and support groups all help, but no matter what they say or do, in the end, it is up to us to cope.

We can list hundreds of reasons to be strong, not to cry, and not to give in to the grief. Yet our bodies, our souls, and our minds eventually demand that we do. We need to allow ourselves time to grieve, to mourn, and to express the myriad emotions these tough times elicit. Using your journal as a tool can help tremendously.

Totally private and all embracing, by its very existence it gives you permission to say all the things you need to—to vent your feelings, to make your plans, and to start over again.

A Fresh Start

When you have finally come to the point at which you have put the past behind you, it's time to think of your future and make a fresh start. Use your journal to help you plan for the months and years to come.

Of course, you'll feel some trepidation. It's only normal to approach a new course of action with a little anxiety, but we humans can be at our best in the face of adversity.

Bad Relationships

Relationships with friends and family have the potential to be great or to be the worst things that ever happened to us. When they're good, they're wonderful. We feel fulfilled and content. But when they go bad, it's like our whole world has turned upside down. It's also one of life's reversals.

The closer we were to the person, the more heavily we were invested emotionally, the more it hurts when the relationship ends. This is a most appropriate subject for your journal, particularly if you view it as a learning experience.

You will have other relationships in the future, and you should know what you did right and what you did wrong. You should ask yourself what you would have done differently if given the chance. Then again, maybe no one was at fault. You may have misread the "chemistry" from the beginning. Don't wallow in misery. Get it out of your system with a cathartic journal.

Blood Relatives

We can't choose our family, but we are nevertheless bound to them by blood. We know that, most of the time, family helps when we need it, but we have plenty of examples in which that does not hold true.

You might wish ardently for a good relationship with a parent, sibling, or other relative, but no matter what you do, they may have no inclination to reciprocate. Or you may experience the opposite situation in which you find that certain relatives act in unacceptable ways, and you wish to have nothing to do with them.

Of course, include these concerns in your journal and deal with them the best way you can. Tell why you do or don't want the relationship. If you can find no good reason to pursue a relationship, then abandon the connection and move on to other, healthier associations. Say as much in your journal and give yourself some credit for strength of character.

When Friendships Die

When a friendship dies, it feels as though the person with whom we had the relationship has passed away. Their absence from our life is just as sudden and almost as final, particularly if either party has determined to cut off all contact. You will mourn the loss of the relationship for a time but will soon recover, especially if you're an outgoing person who makes new friends easily.

Use your journal to get through this time when you miss the morning phone calls or the long conversations over a cup of coffee or when you would love to be watching the football game on TV together. The best way to get over these feelings is to express them. Write about them and don't be ashamed to say how much you miss that person. Consider writing an unsent letter to your friend. Remember the old relationship for what it was and move on. Make new friends and begin new relationships.

Everything for a Reason

At the time we experience a loss, we sometimes think that the absolute worst thing has happened. The loss of a loved one or job causes us to mourn. We see things differently, and try as we might, we can't recapture the past.

The best you can do is accept the loss, complete with its emotional fallout, and deal with it as best you can. Of course, you should turn to friends and family for help or seek out support groups for guidance. But in the end, you are left alone with your thoughts. Don't let them languish. Don't let them disappear into nothingness. They, like you, have worth and should be recorded.

Use your journal as a confidante, a friend, and your other self. Rail at those who would cause you such pain. Cry out from your heart within its pages. Then square your shoulders, hold your head high, and move through life with grace.

The Least You Need to Know

➤ The final good-bye can be the hardest of all, but a journal can help you articulate the many intense emotions.

➤ When a marriage ends, we experience the same feelings as when a loved one dies.

➤ Loss of job can mean a loss of identity for many people. A journal can help you find yourself and find your way.

➤ Bad relationships with family and friends can cause devastating emotional trauma. Using your journal as a confidante can aid you in deciding what to do about those relationships.

Chapter 20

The Glitter of New

In This Chapter

➤ Appreciating the new things and people in our lives

➤ Writing about new relationships

➤ Planning for and recording new adventures

➤ Reliving new experiences in our journals

➤ Testing new thoughts and ideas

New things, new thoughts, and new perspectives add a little lift to our life. They get us out of the everyday rut, refresh our outlook, and recharge our batteries. We all like a little variety now and then, and we look to new things and different surroundings to add a little glitter to our lives.

Whether we are contemplating a new relationship or considering buying a new car, there are lots of things we need to think through before taking the plunge. And once the plunge has been taken, we will always have to deal with certain things. So go on, consider taking the plunge into the new, and don't forget to take your journal with you!

We Are Not Alone

Relationships, whether strictly platonic or wildly romantic, can bring us both joy and heartache. Yet, despite the potential for pain, we seek new relationships to enrich our life, always hoping that the happiness they bring will outweigh the tears.

As you've surely figured out by now, your journal can be used to "test the waters" of any new relationship, to bounce ideas around, and to share the pleasure or pain that our connections bring us.

Reading People

Think about some of your friends and how you met them. Did you like them immediately? Was there something you picked up on with the first hello that told you that you could enjoy spending time with them? By the same token, have you ever met someone whom you immediately distrusted? Have you met someone you didn't like at the outset but then grew to appreciate and enjoy?

Words of Wisdom

"Every human being has, like Socrates, an attendant spirit; and wise are they who obey its signals. If it does not always tell us what to do, it always cautions us what not to do."

—Lydia M. Child, abolitionist and author

Meeting new people is often an exciting and nerve-wracking experience. We often experience contradictory emotions about the people we meet and are never sure where we stand with them or how much we can and should trust them with our friendship.

One of the ways you can help sort out what you're experiencing is to write about the people you meet in your journal. Describe what they look like, but go below surface as well to reveal how they act, if they seem content or unhappy, if you feel like you could trust them, and so on. Describe your conversations and activities, what you have in common, and where you differ. Do you enjoy your time together? If you have any misgivings, write about them, too, and consider them carefully. By writing about these new experiences in your journal, you will be able to gain a better perspective on the relationship.

When It Goes Right

When things happen the way they should and you decide that this is a person with whom you share common values and ideas, it could be a wonderful relationship. As you continue to write about it in your journal, this person will blend from a new friend into an old one.

Just think how great it would be in 10 years to go back and read about how your friendship began. In fact, a copy of some of those early entries might make a wonderful birthday gift.

When Cupid Strikes

Just as you sense that someone might make a good friend, you also can feel a certain "chemistry" when you meet someone with whom you could fall in love. Your heart pounds. Your breathing grows shallow. Your palms sweat. Your knees grow weak. Before you actually take any steps to pursue a relationship with this person you can explore in your journal the pros and cons of being involved with him or her. If one or the other of you is attached to someone else, perhaps you'll only explore the "relationship" in your journal. Either way, go home and write about all you hope for in your journal.

New Places

We all need a change of scenery now and then, and when we choose to go to an entirely new place, it's that much more exciting. You may have no idea what to expect or how the people will be. Take the time to enjoy it at every stage, from idea to realization to aftermath.

The Idea

No one knows for certain what sparks an idea. Out of the blue you may think, "Gee, I'd like to go to Montana," or "I'd like to try out the lake an hour up the road." Who knows what brings such a thought to mind, but the fact remains that you thought of it and it took hold of you, so you begin to make your plans.

The Write Idea

A log journal (see Chapter 6) works particularly well for planning a trip as well as chronicling your journey and recording your afterthoughts.

You research, make phone calls, and ask friends about your destination, all in the process of gathering information. Your journal is the perfect way to record it all in one place so you have it all at hand when you need it.

Everything in Place

Once you have all your plans made, don't sit back like a bump on a log waiting for your departure date. Let yourself experience the anticipation. Learn to enjoy a few little butterflies of expectation. In your journal, write about this and all the things you expect to see and experience. Make a plan for how you want to spend your time. Let the anticipation grow and enjoy this time leading up to your new experience.

Along with your plans for sightseeing and other activities, make sure you work in some time to kick back and relax. The quiet time will give you the opportunity to do some serious thinking and will provide the time for great journal writing.

Out in the World

When you finally arrive, allow yourself to see everything with the eyes of a child. Don't act like the jaded adult that so many of us have become. Ooh and ah at the architecture, natural wonders, or paintings on the museum wall. Marvel at the intricacies of the engineering and wonder about the person with the intelligence and foresight to create such a thing.

Remember all these things until you can get back to your journal and record them. It will be your way of reliving these marvelous days when you saw El Capitan for the first time or stood inches from a Remington sculpture. Of course, you'll write about what you saw, but don't forget to record what you felt and what you thought.

Afterthoughts

Sadly, the new doesn't last for long, and we must return to the usual. Now is the time to sort through your feelings and the things that stood out in your mind. What sight captured your attention? What person do you remember best? What event stands out from the rest? Would you like to make a return visit? Would you like to plan something similar for another time?

Answer all these questions and more in the days and weeks after you return home. Expressing all these thoughts will be like reliving the experience and will burn the event more deeply into your memory.

New Stuff!

One reason people love to shop is the attraction of new things. You can frequent the same stores at your favorite mall every week, but because each merchant takes in new merchandise all the time and moves the old items around, you get a feeling of newness. It doesn't last forever, but the respite is like a short vacation before you go back to your daily routine.

How nice, then, that we occasionally get something new, such as a new car or a new outfit, or encounter a new form of entertainment that makes us laugh. When we find the novelty that brings us a little short-lived happiness, we should take special note of it in our journal so we can revisit it whenever we feel like it.

Little Things Count a Lot

We all crave something new now and then, and it doesn't have to be big or expensive to spice up our lives. A new book or CD can lift your spirits. You can always find something to fit your mood and add a little variety to your life.

Perhaps your favorite shirt has seen better days, but you know where to get another just like it. Maybe you need a new briefcase because your old one is ready to fall apart. Treat yourself to something new. It's fun. Enjoy it. Then write what you like about the new item and how it lightened your mood.

Giving to Others

What works even better than getting something new for ourselves is to find a small gift for someone else. It doesn't have to be a special occasion like a birthday or anniversary. Call it a "just because" gift. Making someone else smile always makes your own spirits soar.

Here is a short list of small items that make great gifts:

➤ A book

➤ A pen

➤ A tape or CD

➤ Homemade cookies

➤ A framed photograph

➤ A fancy letter opener

➤ Candy

➤ Flowers

➤ Favorite foods

➤ Hobby items

Use your creativity and imagination to add to the list. You know your friends and family well, what interests them, and what makes them smile. Help make their day brighter and feel the warmth that lasts far longer than if you did something for yourself. Write about their reaction and how it made you feel. Then make a note to do it again soon.

Putting Pen to Paper

You could also pass along a kind word instead of a material gift. No matter how often a woman hears that she has beautiful eyes, she loves to hear it again. Tell someone you love him or her. That keeps the relationship like new. Keep a list in your journal of nice things you could say to a particular person and then check them off as you pass along your verbal "gifts" to them. That would be something new for you and maybe something new for them as well.

Big Things Count, Too

Bigger things like houses and cars also count in life. The thought of a new car or house may cause financial concerns, but at the same time, we cannot help the excitement we feel at the prospect.

Like a child in a candy store, we test drive cars and search through homes. We consider all the angles and then make a decision to buy or not to buy. You should record the entire process in your journal so that, next time, you can call upon it to review the lessons learned.

Check Out the New Digs

A house becomes a home, a place where you dig in your heels and say, "This is where I belong." You sleep better, eat better, and relax better at home than anywhere else. You have your favorite pillow and don't feel sheepish about putting your feet up on the furniture.

Periodically, events make it necessary to leave a familiar place behind and move to another house. It's an exciting time when we think about the new arrangement of our furniture, new schools, new church, new neighbors, new friends, new everything.

You may have ambivalent feelings about leaving the old and comfortable behind and moving to a new place, but if you think of it as an adventure, you'll enjoy it.

The Write Idea

If you know people who are building or remodeling a house, why not give them a journal so they can record their progress? Consider buying a journal with a blank cover so they can affix a photograph of their home on the front.

A Brand-New House

If you've built a brand-new house, you've had the opportunity to add the little touches to make the place uniquely yours. You get to choose wallpaper, paint, carpet, appliances, and everything else associated with building a new house.

Dealing with builders can prove frustrating. Trying to explain what you want to craftsmen can leave you exasperated, and before the whole ordeal is over, you may promise yourself that you'll never build a new house again.

While you're dealing with all the problems, however, you also may find the process exciting because you're putting so much of yourself into this structure that will eventually become your home. What you do, what you say, and what you feel all provide excellent subject matter for your journal. Be sure to take pictures during the building process to put in your journal. By the time the house is built, you could have a step-by-step pictorial record of the house being built to accompany your written record.

In years to come, you'll be able to go back and read about the trials and tribulations as well as the triumphs. And the generations that follow will find your account a most interesting education in how we did things in our time.

A Preloved House

Don't you love the spin that some people can put on things with the use of a word or a phrase? Take, for example, a realtor's use of the term "preloved." What it actually means is that someone lived there before, and the house is not exactly new. It could be two years old or registered with the historical society.

If you have moved into such a house, you'll realize from the outset that someone else had the pleasure of design and decoration before you. Maybe you fell in love with the huge limestone fireplace in the living room, but the rest of the house leaves a lot to be desired, particularly the 20-year-old shag carpet that is so worn it looks like, well, you're not exactly sure what it looks like.

On the other hand, you may have moved into a house that has been well cared for and constantly updated in exquisite taste. In either case, you still want to make it yours.

Have a little fun with your camera before you change anything. Take "before" pictures of all the rooms, particularly those you're going to want to change. When you have developed your pictures, add them to your journal and write descriptions under each. Discuss what changes you'd like to make and then talk about the changes as you make them.

When you have completed your house makeover, take more pictures. Add them to your journal for a complete account of before and after. As for future generations, they'll have an idea of how styles in furniture and lighting changed over the years.

A New Car

New cars, like new houses, bring with them a great deal of excitement as you picture yourself traveling down the highway. New or used, a car that you purchase is new to you, is a change, and you look forward to it. Take pictures of your vehicle with you in it and place them in your journal. Write your impressions of it and how much you like it. Record how much you paid for the vehicle and where the money came from. Won't it be a treat, years from now, to recall how relatively inexpensive vehicles were?

I mean, think about it. Wouldn't you love to have a picture of yourself in the first new car you ever bought? Or a picture of yourself in the family car when you were 10 years old? Of course you would. You have the opportunity to make a record of today. Do it.

Other News

The glitter of new comes at us from all directions in our personal as well as professional life. We join new organizations, have original thoughts, and take on new jobs. Each comes with a whole variety of new responsibilities, people, and feelings.

We rearrange our life out of necessity or simply because we choose to. In any case, these new things bring novel experiences into our life, and we grow from each of them.

A New Job

On the first day of any job, you don't even know where the rest room is, much less where to find the water cooler. You want to make a great first impression on your co-workers, and no matter how expert you are, you also know that someone will have to answer certain questions for you.

You want to present yourself in your best light but may also have self-doubts. That's normal; just don't voice them. Instead, write about them in your journal. Say whatever you have to say about your anxieties. Get them all out of your system and then show up at the new job wearing your confidence like a brand-new suit.

If you have no doubts, I applaud your sense of self and urge you to write about your self-assuredness as you go into your new job. Write about your new responsibilities and the people you meet. Tell how you like your new position and perhaps if you'd like to stay with this company.

Take the time to write about anything associated with this new job as well as your hopes for the future. Five years from now it could make very interesting reading.

The Write Idea

Service organizations offer an excellent opportunity to meet new people as well as to contribute to your community.

New Associations

We join organizations because we feel we have a lot in common with the people in them. Antique car owners join antique car clubs. Writers join writers' clubs. Community-oriented people join service organizations. In each instance, we form friendships.

When you join a new organization, I suggest you write about it, telling all you know about this particular club and what you hope to accomplish by joining. Perhaps you feel you have something of value to offer and, in turn, begin some new friendships or contribute to the community in some way.

Who knows if such organizations will exist a hundred years from now? Your entries on the subject could prove most educational for generations to come.

Original Thought

When many people believed that the earth was flat, it took a great deal of courage for Christopher Columbus to come forward and say that the world was, indeed, round. He suffered ridicule and disdain from those around him, and yet he pushed onward to pursue his dream.

You may not face the same obstacles that Columbus did, but you, too, encounter the opportunity to fly in the face of convention every day. You can do so not only with your words but with your actions.

Against the Tide

When your co-workers show contempt for someone simply because he or she is new, you can come forward to offer support and friendship. When everyone in the lunchroom announces his or her intention to vote for a particular person you know to be wrong for the job, you have it within your power to voice your opinion.

New thoughts and new perceptions are always difficult for the rest of the world to deal with, but if you have thought them through carefully in your journal first, you will know you have a solid case to present. Whether or not you persuade others to join your point of view is not important. That you came forward with the courage of your convictions is. Give yourself some credit for character in your journal.

A Ground Swell

On the other hand, if you offer a new concept or idea that others immediately embrace, consider yourself lucky. Talk about your new idea and discuss it openly with others. Debate it. Accept the disagreement of others with grace, and of course, there will be some. There always is.

But accept the fact that most people love your idea and write about that in your journal. Try to figure out why they like it so much. Does it solve a problem for them? Can it increase their wealth? Does it make a task easier? Can you think of another idea that will be even better?

Write in your journal about the acceptance of your idea and how it makes you feel. Credit yourself with creativity and then challenge your journal to help you think of another great idea.

A New Anything

New cars, new houses, and new thoughts all make life a little more interesting and, in some cases, even encourage us to grow. We should never miss an opportunity to take what we can from any situation to find enjoyment in life or to improve as a person.

The Least You Need to Know

➤ Writing about new things in life helps us to appreciate them and to experience them again and again.

➤ Describing new relationships and all the emotions that come with them helps us gain perspectives on them.

➤ Planning new adventures in your journal and recording your experiences is a way to keep the trip alive long after it's over.

➤ Use your journal to work out new ideas or concepts that you may have. After you've shared them with the world, write about your experience.

Part 4

How to Write

How you write is as important as what *you write. Your choice of words, your sentence structure, and your rhythm all contribute to the quality of your work. All of these work together to make your journal more interesting and more readable. For that reason, you should take your time with each entry and think as much about how you write as what you write. In time, you'll notice your style improving and your interest level rising. Just like a great novel, your own story will be one that will keep you turning pages and anticipating what will happen next.*

Chapter 21

Elements of a Good Journal

> ### In This Chapter
>
> ➤ You as the main character in your journal
>
> ➤ Writing your journal like a good novel
>
> ➤ Tips for good writing
>
> ➤ Recording dialogue in your journal
>
> ➤ Including rich descriptions and emotions

Imagine, if you will, your great-grandchild sometime in the future settling down to read a good book one quiet evening. A fire blazes in the fireplace, and she has kicked off her shoes to get more relaxed. As she begins reading this marvelous book, she finds that she cannot tear her attention away from it.

Though nonfiction, it reads like a novel complete with wonderful characters and a riveting plot. Now imagine that your great-grandchild is reading your journal. What a heart-warming thought. You can turn this image into reality by using some of the techniques that writers use in creating memorable prose.

You Gotta Have Character

No, you're not writing a novel because, by definition, a novel is a work of fiction. Instead, day by day, you are writing a story of much more importance: the story of your life, with you as the main character.

Your job is to re-create the events of your life and draw readers into your story. Make them care about you as a character in a novel and as a living, breathing person, even though they may be reading your words hundreds of years from now.

You can do this just like a novelist does. You just need a little understanding of how it's done and a bit of guidance to make it great.

From Fairy Tales to Novels

As little children, we loved to hear a good story. Even babies enjoy looking at the pictures in books and hearing the sound of a parent's voice as the tale lulls them to sleep.

Like me, I'm sure you remember stories like "The Three Little Pigs" and "Goldilocks and the Three Bears" when you were very young. As you grew older, you enjoyed more complex plots and the whole spate of fairy tales like "Cinderella" and "Snow White."

Words of Wisdom

"When writing a novel a writer should create living people; people not characters. A *character* is a caricature."

—Ernest Hemingway

Words of Wisdom

"Listen, little Elia: draw your chair up close to the edge of the precipice and I'll tell you a story."

—F. Scott Fitzgerald

I can remember the first time I heard these tales. I got wrapped up in the story, wondering what would happen next to the characters. Be honest: I'll bet you can remember much the same thing about yourself.

As you grew up to enjoy more sophisticated stories, you also fell in love with more complicated characters. Now, when you read a book, you keep turning the pages to learn the next plot development as well as what happens to the characters, and some of these characters are most memorable.

Caring for Characters

Characters are what we care about in a book, a movie, or a television show. It's why we keep turning the pages and why we tune in every day at a certain time on a certain channel to witness the next plot twist and its effect on the people we've come to care about.

Think about *Gone with the Wind*'s dashing Rhett Butler and larger-than-life Scarlett O'Hara, two of the most famous characters from American literature. As complex and complete as any living persons, they are a jumble of emotions and motives with strengths and weaknesses just like us. In fact, when we recognize little bits of ourselves in them, we call that identification.

Nowhere in *Gone with the Wind* does author Margaret Mitchell tell us what kind of people Rhett and Scarlett are. Instead, she shows us through their actions and words. And because they are so human, we care about them. We want to read more. That is exactly what you have to do when you write about yourself and others in your journal.

In the Spotlight

You, as the main character of your journal, have it so much easier than any novelist. You don't have to create a flesh and blood person; you only need to write about one who already exists—you! And you know yourself better than anyone, right?

You, too, can portray yourself as a memorable character, but you'll star in your journal rather than in a novel. Bring out all your wonderful qualities and reveal yourself through your words. You can help your readers love you and want to know all about you.

The Write Idea

Margaret Mitchell published *Gone with the Wind* in 1936 and received a Pulitzer Prize in 1937. It was one of the best-selling novels of the twentieth century and continues to sell very well.

How Tall Are You?

I had a friend in high school, a beautiful girl and honor student who played on the basketball team. At six foot, this taller-than-average young lady had more offers for dates than she could handle. I never gave it a second thought years ago, but now I wonder if her great-grandchildren will ever know how tall she was, that she wore her brown hair chin length, or that every guy within a half-mile melted when she smiled.

Don't let your great-grandchildren speculate about such things. Talk about your physical attributes in your diary. Tell how tall you are and how much you weigh. Describe the color of your eyes, your hair, and how you like to wear it. Attach a photograph.

Putting Pen to Paper

Some new processes and papers have come onto the market recently that supposedly make color photos last as long as any black-and-white photograph, but no one can know for certain for several years. I suggest you keep your negatives and include a black-and-white photo for good measure. If you notice any photographs fading, take your negatives to a good lab to make reprints on updated paper with new processes.

Photo Finish

If you include photographs in your journal, don't glue them to the page. Instead, go to a hobby or scrapbook store and purchase photo album corners. You know, those little glue on corners that you slide photos into. Also remember that although color photos give a more vivid and lifelike appearance, black-and-white photos last longer. Color photographs begin to fade after about 20 years.

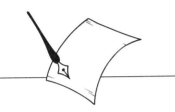

Putting Pen to Paper

Let your vulnerability show in your journal. When others read it in years to come, it will remind them of the common bond between you.

Putting Pen to Paper

Consider all the people you interact with on a regular basis—your spouse, children, family, friends—as the secondary characters of your journal. They, too, have their own stories that intertwine with yours. You might find it interesting to occasionally write a little about their lives in your journal, particularly from the point of view of how it fits in with your life.

Of course, you will change somewhat over time. You'll gain or lose weight. You'll wear your hair differently or have less of it. As time goes by, the overall look of your face may also change. Include updated photographs from time to time.

Main Character

As the main character of your journal, you should reveal your personality as well, little by little, in each entry. No matter what style of journal you decide to keep, you should make sure you write something a little bit out of the ordinary about yourself.

For example, perhaps you went to a movie that you particularly liked. Definitely write about the experience in that day's entry but also add why you liked it. What appealed to you? Did you like it so much because it you got something of value from it? Or did it simply entertain you? Make you laugh? Make you cry? Reaffirm a belief?

Explain how your views have changed over the years and how you have become more patient or more interested in learning. Tell how a certain friendship, book, or chance meeting has affected you. Eventually, you will have presented a complete image of yourself so that any reader in times to come will form a very clear picture of you.

Secondary Characters

Clearly, you do not live in a vacuum. Each day you interact with friends, family, co-workers, and strangers. The people with whom you share a close relationship will appear in your journal regularly, and they present you with a wonderful challenge: Bring them alive within the pages of your journal as you do for yourself.

Describe their physical characteristics as well as how they behave, what they say, and what they do. Write so that anyone reading your words will be able to picture these people and immediately recognize them should they meet.

Show, Don't Tell

Writing coaches and teachers constantly remind students to "show, don't tell." By that they mean don't tell the reader; let the character reveal the trait or emotion. For instance, if someone is angry, don't tell the reader about the anger, show it. Let me give you an example.

> *After their conversation, Tom strode from the room in a fit of anger.*

This simple sentence tells about Tom's emotional state, but it leaves me flat. Tom, the character, hasn't revealed it himself. You could make it much more interesting.

> *"You just don't understand! No one under-stands!" Tom kicked an errant shoe against the opposite wall then strode from the room, slamming the door behind him.*

The second example uses both dialogue and action to demonstrate Tom's anger. The writer didn't have to tell me Tom was angry; he showed me with his actions. With a little bit of imagination and atten-tion to detail, you can do the same in your writing.

Words of Wisdom

"Persons attempting to find a motive in this narrative will be prosecuted; persons attempting to find a moral in it will be ban-ished; persons attempting to find a plot in it will be shot."

—Mark Twain

Spinning a Good Yarn

An interesting plot is another feature of a good novel. Despite Mark Twain's wit in the quotation, his books always had a wonderful plot. Your jour-nal also has a plot, one that life has written for you. You only have to report it.

Granted, you're not going to find a tightly woven narrative as in a novel because life doesn't always happen that way. Your adventures, so much better than any novel, are the stuff of real life, and you are the single thread that runs through it like a glue holding it together.

Putting Pen to Paper

Don't try to structure your jour-nal entries so that they fit into a certain pattern. Write about your life as it happens. The overall pattern will take care of itself.

As you sit down to make your entry, replay your day in your mind as you would a videotape. Think of all the events of the day and pick out the one thing that stands out from the rest. Consider the good and the not so good, the happy and the sad, the people you like and those for whom you have no affection. These are all part of the fabric of your life that, in the end, will reveal a rich and beautiful tapestry.

The Good

It's easy to include happy occasions and the things that make you feel good on any given day. By all means, write about them! They give you and future readers insight into the things that triggered happiness for you.

Write about your roses coming into bloom, your dog having puppies, or your promotion at work. In addition to writing about the event that brought you pleasure, tell why it made you so happy.

The Bad

You can't ignore bad things in life, so don't ignore them in your journal. Don't sweep them under the rug and pretend they don't exist. Write about them in all their gory details. No one will think ill of you. You'll just affirm your membership in the human race. Besides, writing about such things is cathartic and makes us feel so much better.

The Ugly

Sometimes people are rude. Sometimes things happen to inconvenience us. By and large they're not tragedies, though admittedly we'd be happier if they'd not happened at all. But they do happen, and despite the fact that they grate on our nerves, we have to cope.

Don't waste your time agonizing over such things; deal with them. Sometimes the best way to handle such situations is to ignore them. Don't lash out at the stranger who utters a rude remark. Walk away and leave him to his ill temper. Very likely, you'll never see him again.

I know it will bother you all day until you get to write about it in your journal. At that point, unleash everything you wish you had said or done within the pages of your diary. Rant and rave and tell people exactly what you think of them. And when you feel you've said enough, walk away and forget about it.

The Write Idea

Just the right amount of detail can serve to enhance your writing, while too much will slow the story down and detract from the "plot."

The Devil Is in the Details

How much detail you include depends on you. Of course, you have to include enough to make the situation clear to a reader; however, take care not to get bogged down in the little things. Don't include information that has no relevance. Don't try to explain everything you know about a person or a situation. Give the essentials. These are journal entries, not book chapters. Keep it simple.

Keep your writing clear and concise with just enough detail to make it vivid. Sure, you can mention that someone wore a red sweater in order to paint a clearer image, but you don't have to describe every other piece of clothing the person wore. On the other hand, don't discuss a person's family tree if it has nothing to do with the story you're trying to tell.

Keep It Moving

"How did you like the movie?"

"It moved too slow."

Sometimes an otherwise good movie or book gets bogged down by some little subplot or goes off on another subject that has nothing to do with the plot. In fact, you could cut out these parts without affecting the story in any way. Such a cut would move the plot along, strengthen it, and make it more satisfying to the audience.

Be very much aware of this when you make your journal entries. Each entry is a small chapter in which every bit of information needs to hang together from a common thread. That is, it revolves around a single situation, person, event, or thought, with you in the center ring.

If you choose to write about a second event that occurred that day, fine, but start a new paragraph or leave a short space between thoughts. Each event you write about should remain a self-contained entity.

Words of Wisdom

"Dialogue should simply be a sound among other sounds, just something that comes out of the mouths of people whose eyes tell the story in visual terms."

—Alfred Hitchcock

Making Conversation

In real life, people reveal much about themselves and their thoughts by their words. Listen carefully to how people speak, the words they choose, and how they structure their sentences. They also tell us about their attitude by what they do while they speak. Action and dialogue work hand in hand to tell us about the character, a technique you can use to enrich your journal and accomplish three things:

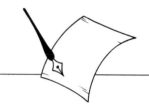

Putting Pen to Paper

Imagine what life would be like without conversation. Include dialogue in your journal to make it more lifelike.

➤ The method will more vividly dramatize the event.

➤ It will help you remember the event more clearly in years to come.

➤ It will draw the attention of future readers and keep their interest at a higher level.

Let me show you what I mean. An entry without dialogue might read like this:

Mary and I met for lunch. She said she didn't know which job she wanted to take, so I told her to think about all her options.

Add dialogue and you get a very different feel:

"I've been offered two jobs," Mary said today when we met for lunch. "They're both great jobs with good pay and benefits, but I'm not sure which one I should accept."

I took a bite of my ham and cheese sandwich and gave my answer a moment's thought. "Maybe you should make a list of each job description, what each offers, and what the opportunities are for advancement."

See what I mean? Which description would you rather read? Don't make anything up. Remember that your journal is nonfiction. Report what really happened.

True Enough

Of course, when I get to the part about dialogue in my workshops, people invariably ask, "How accurate do I have to be when writing dialogue?"

I answer, "Make it as accurate as you can remember."

Contrary to what some people may wish or believe, we don't have little tape recorders whirring around inside our brain, taking down every word exactly as it's uttered. We're not designed that way. However, we do have the ability to recall a conversation with a degree of accuracy that, while changing a word here or there, does not change the meaning.

When writing dialogue, add action tags to record what the speaker was doing at the time. Even if he was standing stock still with his arms crossed over his chest, describe that. Remember you want to paint a vivid and accurate picture.

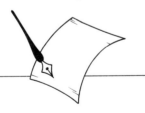

Putting Pen to Paper

You can never remember dialogue exactly as it happened, but you can remember it with some degree of accuracy. Write it as precisely as you can remember.

Proper Format

When writing dialogue, remember the proper format. Let me give you a few easy rules to use as a guide.

➤ The punctuation goes inside the quotation marks.

"Let's go to lunch."

"Would you like to come to the store with me?"

➤ If you add a "tag," it carries its own punctuation outside the quotation marks.

John said, "Let's go to lunch."

"Would you like to come to the store with me?" Mary asked.

➤ Adding an action tag increases interest.

John poked his head through the office door and said, "Let's go to lunch."

Or …

"Would you like to come to the store with me?" Mary asked as she opened the door.

As you can see, you have options for how you present dialogue. The preceding rules are not all of the rules concerning quotations, but they are the most commonly used and probably all you'll ever need. Just be sure to use quotation marks around the words that someone actually said.

Use dialogue as a very powerful tool in relating an event as well as in giving the reader insight into the speaker's attitude, emotions, and even state of mind.

A Life's Tale

Narrative is nothing more than storytelling, an art that has been with us since the earliest humans developed the means to communicate. From prehistoric campsites to Nobel Prize–winning works, we have honed and refined the art into a sophisticated way of relating stories. But at the heart of it all, even the finest novels, is the story.

Your journal, your story can tell a wonderful tale in beautiful language if you write it from your heart and soul, if you paint pictures with your words, and if you portray the emotion you felt.

Words of Wisdom

"With a tale, forsooth, he cometh unto you; with a tale which holdeth children from play, and old men from the chimney corner."

—Sir Philip Sidney

Sensory Description

In Chapter 6, "The Log," you read a little about sensory description, writing about your experiences through your senses. After all, our senses enable us to understand the world around us. Without them, how would we know the color of the sky or the feel of a leaf? Always include some sensory information in your journal entry.

Tell how something felt, looked, or tasted. Don't forget to describe the sound of the music or the smell of the food. You were there. You know what it was like, but how

Words of Wisdom

"Write till your ink be dry, and with your tears
Moist it again, and frame some feeling line
That may discover such integrity."

—William Shakespeare

The Write Idea

Emotion comes from deep within us. Some of us are quite good at hiding what we feel, and no one will know unless we tell him or her. Let your journal be the means by which you tell generations to come.

can you possibly remember it all? You can't. Let your journal remember it and take it into the future for you.

Writing with Emotion

In addition to the senses, emotions prompt us to react to our experiences. All the vivid description in the world will have little impact unless we add the emotions we felt at the time. Remember, the best writing is emotional writing, and you always need to add that aspect to your entries.

While you want to portray the situation accurately on paper for yourself, you also have a second goal: to keep in mind anyone who might read your journal in the future. These are the people you want to step into your shoes, to see what you saw, to feel what you felt.

You want to make them laugh with delight and cry with sorrow just as you did. You want them to feel the doubts and know the certainty.

Make a Strong Foundation

The elements we've talked about in this chapter form the basics of any book people will want to read. Surely, with all the time and effort you invest in your journal, you want it to have all the elements that interest readers.

Just as you have to add the proper ingredients in the right proportions to bake a great cake, you must do the same with your diary. Life writes your plot with you as the main character. Add proper portions of secondary characters, description, dialogue, and emotion, and you will have a journal that readers will want to devour.

The Least You Need to Know

➤ Write about yourself as though you were the main character of a novel.

➤ Don't rearrange things. Record things as they occur. Life writes the plot.

➤ Write in your most beautiful style.

➤ Include sensory description and emotion in your entries.

Chapter 22

Elements of Good Writing

In This Chapter

➤ Writing in the active voice

➤ Using strong verbs

➤ All about adverbs and adjectives

➤ Varying your vocabulary

You can write like a professional. I know you can. Keep certain basics in mind as your hand moves across the page of your book or the keys of your keyboard, and the words from your heart will be the closest thing yet to a time machine.

Vivid writing will enable you to go back and reread entries from years ago and relive a poignant moment or laugh at an old joke as if it were your first hearing. It will give your descendants a clear picture of you and your times and will present you as a real flesh-and-blood person with whom they share much in common.

Good Writing

Good writing is good writing whether you write fiction or nonfiction. I remind my students that a good anything is hard to write but not impossible.

Your Masterpiece

Your journal, a work of nonfiction, is a contemporary record of your life. From day to day you record the true events, the true things that happen to you. You mention the names of real people, and you carefully record true situations. But you want your writing to be as beautiful as possible.

"But I'm not a writer! I can't do this!"

I don't buy it. I've taught enough workshops to know that, with a little guidance, anyone can be a good writer. It doesn't happen overnight, but after all, you're writing every day in your journal. You have years to hone your craft. Give yourself a chance, and you'll see how much your writing improves over time. You only need a few short lessons to help you strengthen your style.

Fixing What's Broken

You've heard the expression, "If it ain't broke, don't fix it." Well, I've changed it a little for the classes I teach. I tell my students, "If you know what's broke, you can fix it."

It's not exactly grammatically correct, but it makes the point. So let's take a look at how to find some of the weaknesses in your style, strengthen them, and make your effort worthy of a literary prize.

Learn from the Masters

I'm sure you have some favorite authors whose books you enjoy, whose stories touch your heart. Read them. Reread them. And then reread them again.

Try to figure out what you like about their styles. Analyze how they present characters and develop plot. Take a close look at their dialogue and how they structure it. Keep reading. Keep analyzing and take some notes on how to do the same thing in your own writing.

Stop! Don't Throw That Book out the Window!

Once in a while, you'll run across a book you think absolutely horrendous. I know I have. Don't throw the book across the room or out the window as you might like to. Instead, take the time to learn from it as well. Figure out why you don't like it.

Is it the writing? Don't you like the characters? Is the plot too thin? Does the dialogue seem stilted? Is the plot too predictable? Does the author use the same word over and over again? You haven't wasted your time reading the book. You will have learned what's broken with another writer's work and can fix it in your own.

Emulate, Don't Imitate

Once you figure out what you like or don't like about certain books and authors, make a point to emulate the good things and avoid the bad in your own writing. Don't imitate, emulate.

If the characters all seem too good to be real, then make sure that, when you write about people in your journal, you present them with their very real human failings. If the plot is too simple and lacks detail, make sure you add a level of detail to your own writing to correct that defect.

Lights, Camera, Action!

A movie without action would be dull enough to put you to sleep. The same holds true for books. You wouldn't want to read anything that bored you enough to send you to dreamland. You should make a special effort with your journal to keep the action moving along and the interest level high.

The Write Idea

When we talk about emulation in writing, we mean to imitate in your own style. As a writer, while you try to write like someone you admire, you will soon find your own style, or voice. Thus, you will move from imitation to emulation.

Keep It Moving

In English, we have something called "active voice." We also have "passive voice." We need both because each serves a purpose, but when you write, take care to write in the active voice as much as possible because it lends movement and vitality to your writing. By the same token, passive voice shows no action and slows down your story. Granted, we need the passive voice, but you should write 95 percent of the time in the active voice for two reasons:

➤ Most readers and writers find the passive voice boring. If you're going to take all the time and trouble to keep a journal, you certainly want to make the writing as exciting as possible.

➤ Writing in the passive voice significantly weakens your writing, while the active voice presents your story with style and force.

Really? What's the Difference?

I once had a workshop participant say to me, "I really don't see any difference between active and passive voice. The same thing happens. The story doesn't change."

I have to concede that the basics of the story remain the same whether you write in active or passive voice. However, don't forget one very important thing: In the passive voice, you're not really sure who commits the action. You only know the receiver of the action. Let me give you a simple example:

The car was hurled against the building.

In this sentence, we know that something dramatic happened to a car and a building, but we have no idea how or why. Despite the possibilities, it's a boring sentence. If we rewrite it in the active voice, however, we learn a lot more, and it's a stronger statement:

> *The tornado hurled the car against the building.*

Now the sentence not only tells me how the car and building met, I can almost visualize it happening. The fact that the tornado caused the action presents a picture of howling wind, rain, and all the accompanying chaos.

Use the active voice as much as possible. With a little practice, you'll be able to immediately recognize the passive voice and learn to change it.

The Write Idea

If you keep your journal on the computer, most programs come equipped with a grammar checker that will point out your passive sentences and tell you what percentage of your sentences are in the passive voice.

Recognizing Passive Voice

You can get quite good at recognizing the passive voice in a short time. Begin by writing your journal entry as you always do. Don't do anything special. And do this in your journal, not on a piece of scrap paper. I think you'll find it interesting to see your writing style develop in the months and years to come when you go back to reread.

When you have finished writing your entry, go back and circle all the words that come from the verb "to be." That is, circle all of the following words: *is, am, are, was, were, be, being, become,* and *becoming*. Likewise, circle *appear, seem, seems like,* and *looks like* when you come across them in your writing. While not passive verbs, they do not portray the strongest meanings. They're tentative at best. Circling the passive verbs will tell you which sentences you should change to the active voice.

Great Changes

Picking out the sentences you need to change is half the battle. The other half comes with the actual changes. This is not rocket science. You have a command of the English language, and you can learn to do this. Let me show you how.

Take a look at this sentence in the passive voice:

> *Regina was saddened by the news.*

Try changing it to ...

> *The news saddened Regina.*

Let's try another:

> *Tony was injured by the falling rock.*

Now you try it.

The correct answer ...

> *The falling rock injured Tony.*

Now go back to the entry where you circled all the passive verbs and rewrite it in the active voice just below it. Play with the language. Think of other wonderful ways to manipulate the words to stronger, more active verbs, and do it all in your journal.

Have fun with it. Create goofy, nonsensical sentences and give yourself a chuckle as you learn. You will see your skills grow from day to day. I can think of no better place to record your growth as a writer than in your journal.

Add Horsepower to Your Writing

If you get rid of your weak, passive-voice verbs, you have to put something in their place. You want to substitute strong, active verbs, but what are they? The verbs you should use show action and should support your whole sentence.

Just as all horses do not look the same, act the same, or have the same strengths, the same holds true for verbs. A farmer would much prefer the strength and stamina of a Clydesdale to the beauty and frailty of a thoroughbred. Both are fine horses, but each has its own particular strengths. While a Clydesdale wouldn't win the Kentucky Derby, a thoroughbred couldn't handle the load of its working cousin.

In the same way that a farmer chooses the stronger breed for work, make sure you use the strongest verbs as the backbone of your writing. Let me give you some examples of Clydesdales:

➤ Talked   ➤ Said

➤ Walked   ➤ Computed

➤ Shunned   ➤ Jogged

➤ Read   ➤ Catapulted

➤ Wrote   ➤ Typed

➤ Drove   ➤ Checked

The list can go on forever, but I think you get the idea. Build your sentences around these words, and you will see your style strengthen by leaps and bounds.

The Right Word

I have three rules of thumb when it comes to choosing the right verb:

➤ Make it active.

➤ Put it in the past tense.

➤ Choose a word full of meaning.

English, such a rich language, contains almost a million words and gives you a huge selection of synonyms. For example, take a verb as simple as *walk*. Any good thesaurus will list several alternatives such as *step, tread, stride, amble, strut, stalk, pace, mince, creep, tiptoe, skip, lumber, stamp, toddle, patter, lurch, reel, stumble, limp, hobble, waddle, shuffle*. Each word carries with it a particular meaning. Each word paints its own picture without the benefit of any additions. Let me give you an example:

He walked down the street.

That sentence tells me nothing about how he walked down the street. Did he walk quickly? Did he walk in a leisurely manner? Did he walk with an uneven gait? A more vivid sentence might read ...

He strode down the street.

This presents a picture of someone who knows where he's going and is walking along at a good pace with a purpose.

He ambled down the street.

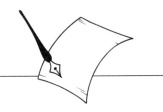

Putting Pen to Paper

If you don't already have a good thesaurus, I suggest you get one and keep it with your journal so you can always choose the best word to express your thoughts.

This sentence presents a whole different picture in which the person walking has no particular urgency to get anywhere.

Learn to look at verbs, action words, as the backbone of the language as well as of your writing.

Picture Words

I remember once a teacher called adverbs and adjectives "picture words" because we use them to paint pictures in the mind. True enough, we use adjectives and adverbs to add spice and color to our writing. They show us number and color and enhance our writing. We can fall in love with them for their beauty. I give you only one word of warning: Don't overuse them.

The Artist's Palette

Adjectives allow you to add color and depth to your picture. They help bring it to life. They give qualities to description and guide readers in what you want them to picture in their mind.

Without adjectives, writing would be sterile and without heart. Let me show you. The following sentence has no adjectives:

> *Stephen wore a sweater, carried a book, and ate a piece of cake while he ambled down the street.*

The sentence, though written in the active voice, has no character. I find the sentence too long, too dreary, and lacking in luster. Let me offer a suggestion to improve it:

> *Stephen wore a <u>red</u> sweater in the <u>cool, autumn</u> weather as he ambled down the street. In <u>one</u> hand, he carried a <u>single</u> schoolbook. With his other, he ate a piece of <u>chocolate</u> cake.*

Do you see the difference? Try doing the same thing with your journal entries. Draw the picture with your verbs and then color it with your adjectives.

The Write Idea

Sometimes you can recognize adjectives by their endings: -er, -est, -able, -ous (such as tall*er*, sweet*est*, and cap*able*).

The "-ly" Song

We need adverbs to add to our already strong verbs, adjectives, or other adverbs by giving us a sense of time or manner. However, just like when using adjectives, take care that you don't overuse them.

Try to avoid words such as *really* and *very*. People tend to use them all the time, making their writing *really very* tedious to read.

Too Much of a Good Thing

Do you have a favorite food? Ice cream? Chocolate? Personally, in my book, chocolate holds a special place as one of the major food groups. In any case, as much as you might love a particular food, you would get tired of it if you had it in large quantities every day.

The Write Idea

We use adverbs to enhance verbs, adjectives, or other adverbs. You can recognize them most *readily* by the -y or -ly at the end of the word. They also give us a sense of time and manner: *We talked <u>yesterday.</u> He <u>quickly</u> explained the theory.*

The same holds true for adjectives and adverbs. Use them to best advantage in small doses, and they will serve you well. Take a look at the following examples:

> *The long blue velvet gown shimmered in the candlelight and dragged behind her on the ballroom floor as she moved toward the dais.*

Cut "long" because it's redundant. By definition, a gown reaches the floor. Then rewrite.

> *The blue gown dragged behind her on the ballroom floor. Its velvet shimmered in the candlelight as she strode toward the dais.*

Remember, you definitely want to paint pictures with your words, but you don't want to mix too many colors together.

Vive la Différence!

The French have an expression that praises diversity: Long live the difference! Obviously, nature loves variety. After all, we have more than 200 species of beetles alone.

We, too, like diversity. Though largely creatures of habit, we seek variation in small ways in all aspects of our life. Not all our clothes are the same color. We don't eat exactly the same food every day. And we like a change of scenery. Why not create differences when we write?

Don't get into the rut of using the same words and phrases over and over and over again. To play it safe, avoid words that even sound vaguely similar within a single entry. Peruse the dictionary. Look through your thesaurus and find different ways of expressing similar thoughts.

As a journaler or a writer, a thesaurus can be one of your most valuable tools. Have it handy when you write or learn to use the one on your computer with skill. It will help you find just the right word.

Write It Right

You want to put forth your best effort in your writing. Knowing the basics of good writing can make all the

Putting Pen to Paper

Listen to how people around you speak. Take particular note of their vocabulary. Most people have a favorite word they use all the time. They use it not only when they speak but when they write.

The Write Idea

When we think of a thesaurus, most of us think of *Roget's Thesaurus*. It was named for Peter Mark Roget, an English physician and philologist known for his *Thesaurus of English Words and Phrases* who died on September 12, 1869, in Malvern, Worcestershire, England.

difference in the world. It can help you strengthen your style by making it more vivid. You can create colorful imagery and guide the reader to step into your shoes to see what you saw and hear what you heard.

Such writing makes the reader laugh and cry and feel all the same things you felt at the time. Give yourself immortality through your words. No one can ask for more than that.

The Least You Need to Know

➤ Keep your words moving by writing in the active voice.

➤ Use adjectives and adverbs but use them sparingly.

➤ Take care to vary your vocabulary as you write.

Chapter 23

Using Your Computer

In This Chapter

➤ Choosing a desktop or laptop

➤ Picking a program

➤ Which peripherals work for you

➤ Keep your filing system simple

Many diarists have turned to computers to keep their journals. If you have access to a computer, you may want to give it a try. You may find you like the ease, convenience, and yes, even portability.

If you don't already have a basic knowledge of computers, you might want to take an adult education class or buy a book to help you out. This chapter assumes that readers have a basic understanding of the concepts of computing.

Choices, Choices

Almost any kind of computer will work for keeping a journal, but certain important choices can enhance your journaling experience and make it easier for you to keep a daily record.

Atop the Desk

If you don't travel very much and contentedly write in the same place every day, then a desktop computer would most likely suit you just fine. Desktop computers, cheaper than their laptop equivalents, usually have larger, easier-to-read monitors.

Because you generally keep desktop computers in one place, it is convenient to keep a printer, a scanner, and other peripherals hooked up to them and ready for use.

The Write Idea

For a fundamental understanding of computers and how they work, try reading *The Complete Idiot's Guide to Computer Basics* by Joe Kraynak.

Likewise, if you have Internet access, you can keep a phone cord plugged into it at all times, ready for the information superhighway!

The downside of desktop computers is that they aren't very portable. As a matter of fact, manufacturers recommend that desktops be moved very little.

Computing on the Go

If you have little room available, travel a great deal, or just like to take your work to the beach or out into the woods, you might consider a laptop. Lightweight (weighing less than five pounds) and portable, these little machines come equipped with substantial RAM, memory, and floppy drives as well as CD and DVD drives.

Current laptops come with larger and easier-to-read monitors than in the past and more comfortable keyboards. They plug into any household receptacle and have batteries that will provide enough power for you to carry on all functions for an hour or two without being plugged in. Thus, you have the versatility of operating, at least for a short stretch of time, without AC power if it's not available.

Anyone who has to work on the go can tell you that the invention of the laptop ranks right up there with chocolate and sliced bread. Laptops allow you to write any time you have a few minutes to spare, and they pack up neatly and quickly into a small briefcase-like bag. Compact and light, you can carry them anywhere.

Although some laptop computers have full-size keyboards and large screens, many still have small keyboards that make typing cumbersome and screens so small that you feel you need a magnifying lens. If you opt for a laptop, I suggest you spend the extra bucks and get a top-of-the-line model that you will feel comfortable using. It'll cost substantially more than the equivalent desktop model but is worth it if you use it a lot.

Side Dishes

While your computer may be your entree, you will want some additional equipment, peripherals, to add to your capabilities. These peripherals, like the side dishes of any meal, will give you variety and enable you to do some interesting things with your journal.

Print Out That Puppy

If you're going to keep your journal or, for that matter, do much of anything on your computer, you have to have a printer. A printer increases your capability to share your work with others by allowing you to print copies of what you've stored on your machine. Of course, you should make electronic backups of all your files, even your journal files, but also print hard copies.

In years to come, computers will have changed so dramatically that anyone finding your electronic backups may not be able to read them on any machine that exists at the time. However, your printed copies will still allow others to read them.

A whole variety of printers exist, from desk jet to laser, from black-and-white to color. It's up to you to decide what you'd like to do and then determine which type to buy. However, if you want to give yourself the most flexibility, I would suggest a color printer of some sort.

Scan It!

Scanners are amazing devices, allowing you to turn your photos, pictures, and written documents into digital files that you can then manipulate, edit, and embed into other files. Just like printers, you can buy black-and-white scanners—though they are disappearing fast—or color scanners. I would suggest a color scanner. This allows you to scan color photographs and documents into your journal pages, which you could then print on your color printer.

Finding the Right Program

Once you've decided on a computer, you'll need to choose a program to keep your journal. The kind of program you use depends on your preferences. Most people find that standard word-processing programs do the job just fine. People can set up the pages as they wish and, since they usually already know how to use the programs, find the ease of operation attractive.

Of course, there are other programs specifically designed for journals. They come with preexisting templates with dates already inserted and thought-provoking questions for you to address. You can find these programs in software stores or on Internet sites. In fact, some sites allow you to download portions of their programs for demonstration purposes.

Word-Processing Programs

Most computers come already loaded with one of the popular word-processing programs, and they work just fine for journal-keeping. You can keep it simple and type on a blank page, or you can create an uncomplicated and straightforward template that looks a little like the one that follows.

Journal of Mary Smith

Date:

Time:

Today's Subject:

Today's Lesson:

You can use the template function of your word-processing program to design it, or save it as an "Auto Text" file, both simple techniques.

Very easy to use, you can back up, type over, or delete, all with a click of your mouse and a keystroke. You can determine the type and size of your font and the overall look of your journal from a menu. It's all very simple, straightforward, and yet powerful.

File It Away

Your filing system should be simple, simple, simple. Consider creating a folder or directory titled "My Journal," for example, in which you can then save another folder for each year's worth of journals.

While you want to keep it simple, you don't want to create a folder with hundreds of individual entries either. I suggest saving each day's entry in monthly files. This will make it easy to find a particular entry when you wish to read it, and it will also keep your filing system manageable.

Here's an example:

My Journal

2000

    January

        January 1

        January 2

        …

        January 31

    …

    December

        December 1

        …

        December 31

2001

    January

    …

If you keep more than one journal, you should also keep multiple folders. For example, in addition to the "My Journal" folder, you might want to have a "My Healing Journal" or "My Spiritual Journal" folder as well.

Journal Programs

Several journaling programs are quite good, but I encourage you to do a little research to decide which one works best for you. They have standard features as well as extras that may be of interest, but be sure to research these programs before you decide to buy one. Ask other journalers which programs they use and which they recommend. Go to Internet sites and download demonstration programs that you can try before buying. Some may have more features than you could ever hope to use, while others may be relatively simple.

One popular journaling program is *1ˢᵗ Journal*, which has everything that a word-processing program does, including a variety of fonts and editing capabilities, and has additional features as well. It offers password protection and data encryption, and you can search for a particular date or subject. You can download a demo copy to try out free for 21 days. Simply go to nextword.com/1stjournalprod.htm and follow the directions on the page.

In addition, you can find another list of journal software sites at journals.about.com/cs/software/index.htm. Each site offers demos that you can try out at your leisure to decide which one you like best.

Give yourself time to make an informed decision. No one is pushing you into anything. Try the word-processing program for a time. Try a journaling demo for a time. Talk with other journalers and then make your decision. But remember, nothing is written in stone. You can always change your mind.

Fancy Features

Whether you choose a journal program or a word-processing program, there are a few features you should look for to enhance your journaling experience. The standards are a spell checker, grammar checker, thesaurus, and dictionary. Make sure the program has these at the very least.

Is It W-E-I-R-D or W-I-E-R-D?

You want to spell it right, but somehow, after a long day, you're not quite sure how to spell a word or two. Unless you choose to use another word instead, you need to check it out. You could grab your dictionary, or you could rely on the spell checker your program provides. With a click of the mouse, your computer will give you w-e-i-r-d as the correct spelling.

When you're finished writing, you can run your document through spell checker, and it will flag any typos and misspelled words and give you options to correct them.

Words of Wisdom

"My spelling is Wobbly. It's good spelling but it Wobbles, and the letters get in the wrong places."

—A. A. Milne

203

What's the Correct Way to Say That?

Don't get too caught up in the grammar of what you write. Let the words flow. After all, you're writing on a computer. You can always go back and change it. However, when you do reread your entry, run it through the program's grammar checker.

It should point out punctuation lapses, spelling errors, misused words, and homonyms. It will not make changes automatically. The program only calls possible errors to your attention letting you make the final decision.

For instance, it will highlight homonyms: *Their you are!* The sentence will show up on your screen and give you options to choose from. Of course, you'll immediately realize you have to make a correction: *There you are!*

You can usually set the grammar checker for a variety of styles from the very casual to the very formal. Some of the more sophisticated grammar checkers offer the specific options of business styles, technical styles, and custom. You choose the one you prefer or customize your own.

The grammar checker will also point out passive verbs if you set it up to do so, giving you the opportunity to make changes. It will tell you when you have misspelled a word or inadvertently repeated a word. In addition, it will give you correct alternatives to choose from.

The Write Idea

In addition to the standard features that your software provides, consider purchasing additional programs as supplements such as encyclopedias and other reference materials. They usually come on a CD that runs in conjunction with your program. You can call it up at any time to make use of it when the need arises.

The Thesaurus

Congratulations! You had a good day, and as you write about it in your journal, you find yourself typing "happy," "happy," and "happy," yet again. If you find the repetition tiresome, imagine what people will think 100 years from now when they read your entry.

Your program should have a thesaurus feature to help you find alternatives for that "happy" word. It should give you a long list that might include, "joyful," "joyous," "merry," "laughing," "glad," and "beaming." The list could go on and on. It should be easy to access with a click of the mouse or a keystroke.

Composing on the Computer

Like most people, if you're new to the computer, you may feel more comfortable writing in longhand first and then transcribing your words onto the computer. Before long, however, your brain will be moving at 100 mph while your hand still only moves at 20 mph. You'll see the necessity of composing on the computer.

Getting Into the Groove

At first, composing on the computer will seem foreign to you, particularly if you don't type fast. However, you'll soon get used to it and will increase your typing speed, even if it's only the hunt-and-peck method.

You'll find that your words flow more smoothly, and you'll wonder why you ever did it any other way. The freedom of letting your fingers fly over the keys is liberating, letting your words and thoughts flow from your brain to the screen with the speed of thought.

The Necessity of Editing

I'm sorry to have to tell you this, but no one ever gets it right the first time out of the chute. While your journal should be a place where you feel free to write however you wish, you'll probably want to go back to fix things here and there after you've gotten everything down. Think of all the times you've filled out a simple form and made a mistake. Consider how often you've written a note and crossed out a word because you thought of a better one. Remember how many times you think and rethink an answer in an ordinary conversation. Yes, you should revise, if only a little.

But take heart. You have a computer. You won't have to rewrite everything. Just a word here, a phrase there, and you'll have written a beautiful piece of prose.

Make It Shine

Refer to Chapters 21, "Elements of a Good Journal," and 22, "Elements of Good Writing," and use all the tips provided as a guide for your revisions. Take it one sentence at a time and ask yourself six key questions:

1. Have I written in the active voice?
2. Do the words I have chosen express my thoughts accurately?
3. Have I written clearly enough so that anyone reading this will understand the situation and how I feel?
4. Have I written vividly or can I substitute a word here or there to make it more so?
5. Is my spelling correct?
6. Is my grammar correct?

As you can see, they're very basic questions. Running your entry through a grammar check will point out any mechanical errors you may have made. Since your entries are probably not more than a few paragraphs long, the whole process will only take a few extra minutes of your time and require very little effort.

Taking It to the Max

The few extra minutes required to edit not only will improve your entry but help you develop better skills as a writer. If, for example, you always find yourself cutting out the word "that," then you will eventually think twice before writing it down the next time.

Spelling and grammar all contribute greatly to style. Continue to hone your skills. Continue to learn the correct form, and you'll see great improvement in your writing over the years.

Creating a Masterpiece

Within your computer, you have the means to make your journal an ever-more-powerful tool. Admittedly, I still don't know everything my computer can do, but I'm still learning and loving it. Take the time to learn the capabilities of your machine.

With the right computer, software, and peripherals, you can make your journal not only read beautifully but look beautiful as well. You can add embedded photos and drawings and print it all out in color. What a book! What a masterpiece! What a gift!

The Least You Need to Know

➤ Choose the right computer to fulfill your needs.

➤ Determine which peripherals will give you flexibility with your journal.

➤ Spend some time researching and trying out programs.

➤ Make sure your program has these standard features: spell checker, grammar checker, thesaurus, and dictionary.

➤ Keep your filing system simple.

Chapter 24

Internet Journaling

In This Chapter

➤ Finding journaling sites on the World Wide Web

➤ Exploring newsgroups and chat rooms

➤ Sharing your journal with the world

Now that you're into the journal groove and have been writing religiously every day, maybe you're ready for something new. If you have a computer and Internet access, why not try out a couple of online journal sites to see what's out there in the world of the Web?

The World Wide Web abounds with sites where people keep a wide variety of journals. The idea may capture your imagination and lead you to participate as well.

Getting Plugged In

To keep an online journal, you must gain access to the Internet. Once you're online, you'll find the many varieties of sites that exist, and you'll have the luxury of picking and choosing exactly the right one for you.

You can find literally thousands of Internet sites devoted to journaling. Some sites have only merchandise for sale; some are designed solely for the purpose of online journals. Others are a combination of the two, and still others are just pages of links that lead you to more sites.

You can find a partial listing of these sites in the appendix at the back of this book, but bear in mind that many more exist, and you can find them easily through links and search engines.

Go to these sites. Read them. See what kinds of journals people put online at each site because you will notice a particular style. Some are very private while others are written in a much lighter vein. Knowing what kind of online journal you'd like to keep will help you decide which site would serve you best.

The Write Idea

The Internet originally began with the intention of providing a means to exchange information among universities and various government departments.

Out of the Closet

Just as there are many styles of traditional journals, you have these same options when you keep an online journal. Of course, you'll keep a particular type (such as a log, an unsent letter, or a reflective journal) as we talked about in earlier chapters, but you must determine what details you wish to divulge about yourself.

The best way to decide the issue is to first read other online journals. Some sites have very personal entries, while others cover subjects of a less personal nature. Visit several sites.

Determine how intimate other writers get at each site and decide which would be most comfortable for you.

Up Close and Personal

If you have a desire to tell the whole world about yourself, right down to your deepest, most closely held secrets, then by all means find a site on the Web and make a place for yourself.

Others will welcome you with open arms, and you may even gain a regular following of readers who will give you feedback via e-mail.

Through your e-mail correspondence, you'll gain a whole new circle of online friends with whom you share common interests and views. Some will differ from you greatly, and you can become involved in some exhilarating online debates. Additionally, it's an easy matter to copy your e-mails and make them part of your journal for future reference.

Cooking the Books

On the other hand, you may be unwilling to bare your soul for all to see, a totally understandable point of view. Perhaps you'll grow into it and perhaps not. If not, you can keep a less personal journal online.

Have you ever heard the expression "cook the books"? It refers to keeping two sets of accounting books: the real books and a set to share with the world. Of course, in the business world, this practice is not only illegal but highly unethical. However, when talking about your journal, two sets of books offers you a very practical alternative. You can maintain a bit of privacy while you keep an online journal in one of two ways.

Your first option is to keep a theme journal as your online journal on a totally separate subject from what you're writing about in your personal journal. For example, if you're renovating your house, you could keep a running account of those activities. If you take language classes, you could write about that aspect of your life. In short, you can choose a subject that is not particularly private but is nevertheless important to you.

Your second option lies in keeping a private journal and then picking and choosing certain parts of your entries to put online. Tell what happened to you. Share where you went and what experiences you had, but decline to write about the more intimate details. Either way is a viable option. You just have to figure out which one you like better.

The Write Idea

Keeping an online journal as well as a more private journal gives you a way to maintain a certain amount of privacy while sharing a portion of your life with everyone else.

Interacting with Other Journalers

Because you give up a certain amount of privacy when keeping an online journal, you may attract the attention of others who may be experiencing the same emotions or situations as you. That's obviously something that doesn't happen when you keep a strictly personal journal.

Journal sites on the Web offer a wealth of interaction with others and information-sharing on a global scale, something never imagined by some of history's most famous journal keepers. The Internet is a wonderful communication tool. Use it.

Into the Forum

Since others can read your journal and perhaps identify with you, you will likely receive e-mail notes from people sharing similar experiences. You may even begin an extended correspondence with these people. They may tell you about other sites or invite you into a chat room to talk with others.

Words of Wisdom

"It's what I always wanted—to be in touch with a community of ideas like this. ... There's something thrilling about the Internet. ... It almost doesn't matter what anyone says. It's more the thrill of knowing you're in touch with people laterally, rather than through a filter of some kind."

—Brian Eno, British rock musician

209

As you correspond with these fellow journalers, keep in mind that they can be from anywhere in the world. However, despite any cultural differences, never forget that people are people the world over. They want and need the same basic things for themselves and their family. They feel the same joys, hurts, and sorrows, and for those reasons, somebody in Australia's outback can share your joy when you journal about your children, for instance.

Let's Have a Chat

Sites and chat rooms where people can sign in to engage in spontaneous electronic correspondence on the subject of journal-keeping abound, so enjoy them. Explore and learn about as many as you can. You will like some instantly, and others will immediately be of no interest to you, while still others will grow on you over time. Give them a chance. Go to the chat rooms. Glean and offer whatever information you can. It's all about sharing.

Once in a chat room, what you talk about depends on the mood and tone of the people there. Some chat rooms have very specific rules, such as if a room is specifically a journal-writing chat room, then people will ask you to confine your remarks to that subject.

Other rooms may have less stringent rules and welcome discussions of any kind. With a little experience in a variety of rooms, you'll soon come to determine which ones you like best and which people you share the most with.

Newsgroups

A newsgroup consists of a group of people on the Net who have something in common such as keeping a journal. They leave messages on bulletin boards for each other to read and respond to. A number of newsgroups devoted to journal writing (and any other subject you can think of, for that matter) exists on the Internet. An excellent place to exchange ideas with other journalers about everything from kinds of paper, books, and software to the best glue to use when adding a comic strip to your journal, you can find some kindred spirits there.

Just as with any other site on the Net, you may choose from hundreds of different newsgroups devoted to journaling. Take your time to explore and discover which ones you like best.

You will most likely make your decision based on the personalities of the people in the newsgroup, just as you would for a chat room. Some groups may overflow with kind and wonderful people who have the desire to share information, while others may be populated by people who prefer to gossip and belittle the efforts of others. You'll be able to determine which groups and chat rooms those are in a few minutes. You'll learn that those sites are not only counterproductive but have nothing of any consequence to offer the serious journaler.

Access

How you access the newsgroups depends on your ISP (Internet service provider). Some allow you to type in a keyword, such as "newsgroups," and an entire menu flashes on the screen for you to choose which newsgroup you wish to explore. Others provide a newsgroup icon that you simply click on. You'll have to determine how to find them on your specific service, but it should be no more than a few easy steps.

If you cannot find them after a little exploration, ask some of your real-world friends, check with your e-mail buddies, or call your ISP's technical support department.

Over the Fence

In years past, housewives shared information, recipes, tips on child rearing, and gossip over backyard fences. Today's newsgroups and chat rooms serve much the same purpose.

On the specific subject of journal writing, you'll find other individuals with whom you can share information about software, techniques, ideas, and even online journals. Some people even keep a journal about their journal idea exchanges. There is so much information that you could spend weeks online and never scratch the surface.

For All the World

Online journaling offers a fascinating new aspect to journaling and is a new development on the Net. Just as no one could have predicted the vast success of the Web, neither could anyone have foreseen the popularity of online journaling. After all, it had been previously thought of as a totally private venture.

Now, however, as the world shrinks and the Net makes instant worldwide communications possible, we feel the need to reach out to people on the other side of the world. We seek out those who love to write and record the events of their life. We find comfort in knowing that people of different cultures share ideas similar to ours. We revel in lively debate when we find someone with a different viewpoint.

My hope for you is that you at least explore the Web as a vehicle for online journaling as well as making contact with people from all over the world. If we all made use of the access afforded us by the Net, we'd all have a better understanding of each other as well as ourselves.

The Least You Need to Know

➤ Because so many journaling sites exist on the Net, you can afford to be picky when looking for the right one for you.

➤ You can write an online journal while maintaining your privacy.

➤ Chat rooms and newsgroups put you in touch with people all over the world. You can share information about journaling and any other subject you choose.

Part 5
Taking Control with Your Journal

Life is a complex proposition, too complicated to sum up in a single sentence or with an all-encompassing concept. In fact, if you look through the shelves of a bookstore or library, you'll find a number of philosophies, some so different from each other it's hard to imagine that they come from the same planet.

Because so many philosophies exist, it's hard to imagine that any one can speak with any meaning to all people of all cultures. And make no mistake, we must all have some philosophy of life to enable us to take joy in the good times and overcome the more difficult obstacles in life. No one can give you an answer, but you can find the answers for yourself. You have the power within you to not only survive, but to shine, excel, and succeed. Use journal writing and its many techniques to take control and thrive.

A Different Journal for a Different Purpose

A journal won't solve your problems, but it does allow you the time and space to find the answers you're looking for. It won't make you a better person, but it does give you a tool to become one if you want to. You have the answers within you. Sometimes all you need is the quiet time to find them. If nothing else, a journal affords you the solitude, the time to consider, and the permission to find what you need from the deepest part of yourself.

Since your needs can change from day to day and week to week, your journaling style and techniques will necessarily change accordingly. Only you will know what you need. Sometimes a single journal will suffice, while at other times, you'll want to keep two or more because of the complexity of your life. Go with the flow and let the journaling muse take you where she will.

For Your Review

Once upon a time, you opened a book or created a computer file with the intention of keeping a journal. You felt a need to record the dearest secrets of your heart and events of your life. Perhaps you wanted to get your thoughts in order. Maybe your religious beliefs led you there.

The Write Idea

Some religions, such as the Mormon faith, encourage their members to keep a diary.

There are as many reasons for keeping a journal as there are people who wish to make such a commitment. But as time goes by, you'll notice that your reasons will change as well as the benefits you derive. To get the most out of your journal, you need to regularly review your reasons and redefine them as necessary.

In previous chapters, you've read about a variety of journal types, and by now, you may be considering what kind appeals most to you. If not, let me make specific suggestions for you to think about when making your decision regarding what kind of journal to keep.

From the Inside Out

For some people, keeping a journal is a religious obligation. Others may think it's just a great way to pass the time. Still others want to keep a journal with the express purpose of leaving a legacy. Whatever your reasons today, they may change tomorrow. That's okay. By the same token, let yourself adjust your style of journal as your life alters. I cannot emphasize enough that you need different things at different times in your life, and you should adjust your journal accordingly.

The following are the types of journals we discussed earlier in this book as well as a brief review of the reasons for each.

The Log Journal (Chapter 6)

➤ Keeping a straightforward, contemporary life record

➤ Keeping a detailed record of events for future reference

➤ Setting goals and working toward those goals

➤ Keeping track of diet and exercise routines

The Healing Journal (Chapter 7)

➤ Managing pain

➤ Recording symptoms

➤ Maintaining a positive frame of mind

➤ Tracking your medication

The Cathartic Journal (Chapter 8)

➤ Venting your emotions

➤ Telling your side of the story

➤ Saying everything you wish to say about a subject

➤ Saying what you wish you had said or done in the past

The Unsent Letter (Chapter 9)

➤ Saying good-bye

➤ Saying things you should have said to a particular person

➤ Expressing regret

➤ Expressing other emotions

➤ Telling someone you miss him or her

The Theme Journal (Chapter 10)

➤ Planning a special event

➤ Recording weeks or months of a continuing activity

The Reflective Journal (Chapter 11)

➤ Exploring your character

➤ Improving your character

➤ Exploring and expanding your code of ethics

The Spiritual Journal (Chapter 12)

➤ Exploring the state of your soul

➤ Exploring your relationship with the divine

➤ Achieving peace of mind

➤ Striving toward a better relationship with the divine

The Family Journal (Chapter 13)

➤ Recording family events

➤ Chronicling family growth

➤ Chronicling children's growth

➤ Recording special family events

The Dream Journal (Chapter 14)

➤ Recording dreams

➤ Helping you analyze dreams

➤ Helping make decisions based on what your subconscious mind is trying to tell you

The Historical Journal (Chapter 15)

➤ Recording events of the past

➤ Giving you a sense of your accomplishments

➤ Helping you compare the past with the present

➤ Making sure you have certain things written down

The Travel Journal (Chapter 16)

➤ Keeping track of mileage and expenses

➤ Recording all the places you went

➤ Writing about people you met

➤ Remembering impressions

The Hobby Journal (Chapter 16)

➤ Recording why this hobby interests you

➤ Discussing how you got started

➤ Describing projects

➤ Keeping track of your increasing skills

The Writer's Journal (Chapter 16)

➤ Recording ideas

➤ Saving great lines

➤ Archiving project beginnings

➤ Developing characters

As you can see, there is a journal type for nearly every activity or need. Now is the time to pick the one you'd like to begin with. Experiment, explore, discover, and then try another. But be flexible and keep writing.

Your One and Only

Whichever type of journal you choose, remember that it most likely will only be your first. Today you may want to keep a log, next week a reflective journal, and two months from now an unsent letter. In any case, you'll probably start out by writing in only one journal. Over time, you may opt to add others, but we will call this first diary your *primary journal*. How you use this will differ to some degree from anyone else who keeps a journal.

Based on personal experience and information others have so generously shared with me, let me offer a suggestion to help you use your primary journal to its best advantage.

Acting on Impulse

Weeks or months may go by without anything out of the ordinary happening. You'll go about your usual routine interacting with family and friends, going to work, paying bills, taking part in various activities, and writing in your journal. But then, out of the blue, something unexpected or extraordinary happens.

Suddenly you need to unburden yourself with an unsent letter, or you need to vent, or something has happened that causes you to consider your soul, and you feel the need to keep a spiritual journal at least for a while. You can use your primary journal for all of these if you so choose.

Day to Day

I call using your primary journal for fulfilling all of your needs the "day-to-day" method because, while the writer addresses a variety of facets of life, he or she maintains a chronicle of day-to-day events, much like a log. Then, when something out of the ordinary or noteworthy happens, you make an additional entry that reflects what you feel. Let me show you what I mean:

> "Work has been very satisfying for me lately. I've been given more responsibility and more opportunities to contribute to the business. John, my boss, made me feel particularly good today when he stopped by my office and told me how pleased he was with my last report."

Then continue with the additional aspect of your life that you feel compelled to write about:

> "Last night, I finished reading a book that has had a profound effect on me and has caused me to think seriously about my life and my contribution to society. I wonder if I spend enough time volunteering at the community center. It has caused me to rethink some of my priorities as well. Do I spend enough time with my family or do I always give them second place after my job?"

You can see where this is going. While the first part of this entry is very much an event-driven journal, like a log, the second part, clearly separated by space and meaning, would be characterized as a more reflective style.

The journal keeper in this instance has only one book but makes multiple entries of different types when the need or desire arises. When the writer has worked through a problem or addressed certain issues to their conclusion, he or she will go back to simply keeping the primary log.

The Catch-All Journal

Ah, the unexpected always has a way of putting in an appearance, and you have to deal with it. You'd like to write about the situation in your diary, but you prefer to keep your primary journal as a record of your everyday life.

Why not buy a second journal or create a second file in your journal directory on the computer? Designate one as your primary journal and the second as your "catch-all" journal. Continue to keep your primary journal as you always have. However, when something out of the ordinary occurs, reach for the second book.

In this second book, you will record all the unusual events, themes, reflections, plans, and meanderings of your mind. For example, perhaps you saw a movie that truly touched you or motivated you to take some action. The fact that you went to the movie is of little note, but the fact that it affected you in such a way is. You would record that in your catch-all journal.

After you have made your daily entry in your primary journal, reach for your catch-all journal and write about how the movie affected you. Describe the movie and your emotions. Discuss what you'd like to do as a result. If you decide to take action, keep a running chronicle of what you do. Maybe you'll meet with some success. Maybe you'll hit a brick wall. In either case, tell what resulted.

Meanderings of the Mind

In addition to unusual or profound events, you might consider using your catch-all journal for seemingly isolated thoughts and concepts that may come to mind.

You might think of a phrase, a word, or a metaphor that crystallizes a whole concept for you. You might get an idea to solve a problem or improve on a way of doing something. All these things are worth writing down. In fact, in the writers' workshops that I teach, I encourage writers to keep such a journal, an idea or writer's journal such as those described in Chapter 16, "Other Types of Journals."

A Dime a Dozen

Ideas may be a dime a dozen, but great ideas come at a premium. We've all had ideas that have caused us to shout "Yes!" because they trigger something in us and we want to act on them immediately. We can't always do that. Instead, satisfy the urge and write it down in your second journal.

Juggling Multiple Journals

A gentleman in one of my workshops sat quietly through the entire presentation making copious notes. At the end when I opened the floor to questions, he raised his hand.

"What if I need to keep more than one journal?" he asked. "I want to keep a personal journal, a business journal, and I really like the idea of a family journal."

Other people in the workshop echoed his sentiments and listed a variety of journals they'd like to keep. For the next 20 minutes, we discussed a way of juggling your journal writing time.

So Much to Do ... So Little Time

Like the gentleman in my workshop, you may want to keep multiple journals. For example, you may want to keep a personal journal, an online journal, an unsent letter, and a family journal.

If you wrote in each one every day, you'd devote a huge chunk of time to writing about your life instead of living it. Just as we schedule time for all our other activities, you can do the same for your journaling. The key lies in scheduling particular days and times to write in each.

The Write Idea

The number and type of journals you keep will vary with your life needs and your imagination. Some people I have met use a varying number of journals depending on what is happening in their life. Some claim to keep as many as five at one time.

What Day Is This?

First designate your primary journal, the one in which you will write most often. Perhaps you'd like to keep to a daily schedule for this diary or change it to an every-other-day time frame. Whatever you decide, keep to the schedule and continue to write in it on a regular basis.

Next decide what other kinds of journals you'd like to keep and formulate a schedule to write in them. For example, if you'd like to keep a family journal, 2:00 on a Sunday afternoon might be an optimal time for you and your family to get together to contribute to that journal.

If you'd also like to keep a weekly business journal, perhaps late on a Friday afternoon would be most appropriate. In addition, if you're facing some unresolved problems that you'd like to bring to a satisfactory conclusion, schedule time for your unsent letter or cathartic journal first thing Monday morning. Add to that an online journal in which you'd like to share information about your garden, and you've got quite an agenda!

Keep It Simple

Don't keep adding journals for the sake of adding them. Keep your journaling as simple as possible. In most cases, two diaries will serve you well enough, but if you find the need for more, then of course keep as many as you need.

Below you'll find a sample schedule that will enable you to keep as many as five journals at one time. It's just a suggestion, but you can use it as the basis for your own timetable.

Sunday:	2:00 P.M.	Family journal
	10:00 P.M.	Primary journal
Monday:	10:00 P.M.	Primary journal
Tuesday:	8:00 A.M.	Cathartic journal
	10:00 P.M.	Primary journal
Wednesday:	10:00 P.M.	Primary journal
Thursday:	10:00 P.M.	Primary journal
Friday:	3:00 P.M.	Business journal
	10:00 P.M.	Primary journal
Saturday:	2:00 P.M.	Online journal
	10:00 P.M.	Primary journal

Putting Pen to Paper

Once you set up a schedule, do your best to adhere to it. It will keep your enthusiasm and creativity at high levels.

As you can see, this schedule allows you to keep five different journals at a time. You write every day for some period of time in your primary journal but in no more than two journals a day.

You're not spending hours chronicling your life; you're living it. In addition, you're writing about and emphasizing different aspects of your life and addressing some issues in detail. It could prove very advantageous to you in working out emotional issues, making plans, or finding out more about yourself.

Besides, in years to come, you may find it most interesting to review these times of your life when things became so complex. You will remember your thoughts and feelings at these times and perhaps draw upon the lessons learned for future problems.

Hybrid Journals

Remember, keeping a journal has two main purposes: to explore yourself and to help you find your mission, your place in the world. Bend your journal to fit your purposes and to help you achieve your aims. To achieve your particular goals, you may decide to use a combination of two or more types of journals.

Your Inner Self

The two types of journals that traditionally deal with self-exploration are the reflective and spiritual journals. Sometimes, however, you might mix them, such as when you're working toward self-improvement or becoming more spiritual. In addition, if you have particular goals you'd like to achieve, such as to become kinder, more generous, or more outgoing, combine the spiritual and reflective style with the log journal.

You can also combine the log with the healing journal. Set goals for yourself regarding your emotional or physical health. For example, if you must take physical therapy to recover from an injury, you could set your goals for recovery. Perhaps that would entail lifting specified weights or walking a set distance.

You could describe your progress after each session and keep focused on your goal. In this particular hybrid, you'd also write about the pain of the therapy, how it made you feel, and how happy you were at your accomplishments.

On the other hand, if you've got emotional issues to deal with, a combination of an unsent letter and a cathartic journal would suit you best. As you address your letter to a particular person, you can unleash all your pent-up emotions by telling him or her exactly how you feel and getting out your side of the story.

You get the idea. Pick and choose characteristics from different types of journals and meld them into something uniquely yours. Use your imagination and don't restrict yourself.

As the Crow Flies

In certain instances in which everything seems to be in turmoil, you can't quite get a handle on things. In these cases, I suggest you throw all the rules out the window. Write whatever comes to mind. Address whichever emotion surfaces at that moment, and your journal will grow to become a conglomeration of many types.

Lessons to Teach

Your life is truly a unique journey. You have important things to say and important lessons to learn, and once you learn them, you will want to record them for your own reference as well as for others.

Only you can express yourself with your words. Only you can speak with heartfelt emotion of the pains and joys of your life. Only you can record what life's lessons have meant to you.

We do not soon forget lessons learned the hard way, but it's a nice moment when we can look back and revisit those times. We find satisfaction in knowing that, despite the obstacles, we have not only survived but flourished.

The Least You Need to Know

➤ Specific journals help you accomplish specific goals.

➤ A single journal can serve your needs with the right technique.

➤ Multiple journals work well when life becomes very complicated.

➤ Hybrid journals grow out of your particular needs.

Chapter 26

From Journals to Philosophy

In This Chapter

➤ How to formulate a life philosophy

➤ Gaining perspective on what's important

➤ Expanding your horizons

➤ Improving your quality of life

➤ Achieving your goals

Throughout this book, we have discussed the history of journals, the different types, what to write, and how to improve your journal writing. Now I'd like to leave you with some final thoughts about journals and how to take advantage of the great power that you have within you.

Your journal can be your tool to help discover things about yourself, enable you to reach out to the world, help others, and guide you in formulating the philosophy by which you live your life.

Formulating Your Philosophy

The longer you keep a journal, the more you will demand of it, and this is as it should be. Just like anything else in life, the more we do it, the better we get at it, and the more sophisticated we grow in its practice.

In addition, the longer you keep your journal, the more you will think about "deeper" subjects, mainly because the mere practice of keeping a journal gives you the time and space to ponder questions beyond the everyday. Everyone develops a personal philosophy as they mature; it's just that most people haven't put a name to it.

You look at life in a certain way. You decide which things are right and wrong based on a code of behavior dictated by religion, law, mores, or ethics. From your knowledge of established and accepted behaviors, you decide on a code of behavior for yourself. You need neither an extensive education nor a degree in law, just a few years of living and life experiences.

The Write Idea

You can base your personal philosophy on the best of what other philosophies have to offer. That philosophy then governs how we perceive the world as well as our behavior.

The Write Idea

Most humanist or secular philosophies claim that values are relative, that is, that certain behaviors are considered wrong in certain instances and right in others. Circumstances play a huge role in determining the right and wrong of any behavior.

Religious-Centered

If you're a religious person, you can draw from the sacred texts of your faith to help you articulate your personal philosophy. Each of the world's great religions has words of wisdom for living life, and they all offer a code of conduct such as The Ten Commandments.

Most religions espouse codes of conduct and claim their values as absolute because they come from a divine and constant source. Others, on the other hand, propose religious philosophies that outline a way of life.

All, however, encourage their adherents to seek spiritual growth and harmony within society. They dictate that certain behaviors are unacceptable while others are desirable. However, none tells you how to perceive the world. That is entirely up to you based on your life experiences.

Has someone behaved correctly toward you in a certain situation? Have you behaved in a righteous manner? Sometimes the answers to questions of this sort are easy, but most often, they border on a gray area that requires a great deal of thought. That's what your journal is for. To debate the different sides of the questions and then decide which one best fits the teachings of your religion or religious philosophy.

Humanist-Centered

If you don't consider yourself a particularly religious person but would rather concentrate on the things of this world, then you would derive your philosophy from other sources such as the law or other philosophers, past and present.

Whether they espouse relative or absolute values, many of the secular philosophers take into account human frailties. While they do not expect perfection, they encourage character growth based on a code of ethics.

Taking Responsibility

Whether religious or humanist, both encourage personal growth and social responsibility. To formulate your philosophy, look carefully at what the religious and humanist viewpoints have to offer. Study each viewpoint. Discuss them with people you know. Write about them in your journal. Describe what appeals to you about each and what you find difficult to comprehend.

Eventually, you will find that you will have constructed a guide to living, or philosophy, complete with a way of putting things in perspective and a code of ethics and behavior.

Gain Perspective

Proper perspective marks you as a wise person. It enables you to recognize the difference between the little things and the big things in life. It gives you the wisdom to know which requires action and which to ignore.

While some things are worth fighting for because of the principle they represent, we need to let many of the small things pass by without so much as a nod of recognition because, well, they're just not worth it. Sometimes it's hard to make the call, but using your journal as a sounding board and your personal philosophy as a guide, you can determine which course of action is most appropriate in any given situation.

The Little Things

"But, Mom, I want to wear the purple shirt with the brown pants."

This particular color combination may not be your favorite, but do you want to have a knock-down-drag-out fight with your child over it? Probably not, particularly if both articles of clothing are clean and age appropriate. Typically, these little tiffs occur when your child is three or four years old and wants to do everything "by myself." So you make a face to show your displeasure and let the child wear the odd combination.

I remember when my three-year-old decided to wear a long-sleeved red shirt with purple shorts and put her sneakers on the wrong feet because that's what she wanted to wear on that day.

At the grocery store, a woman approached and said to my daughter, "I'll bet you dressed yourself this morning."

My daughter beamed while I asked the woman, "How did you know?"

She said, "I raised four children, and they all had a 'different' fashion sense." She chuckled and went on her way down the aisle.

In this instance, my daughter expressed a certain amount of independence and creativity in her choice of clothing. I may not have agreed with it, but it did no harm and, in fact, was a positive experience for her. I chose not to fight about this little thing.

Things Worth Fighting For!

On the other hand, life often presents us with situations of much more import. They draw our attention because, based on our life's philosophy, we see them as inappropriate or wrong. Some things are worth fighting for, such as when you see an injustice or when a political candidate with whom you greatly disagree is running for office.

In these instances, you should work to correct the injustice or give your support to a candidate who more closely mirrors your own philosophy. When you write in your journal, state your intentions to do something about the things you wish to correct. Tell why you want to get involved and how this relates to your philosophy. Describe your efforts and their results.

Keeping your journal in such a way will constantly reinforce your philosophy and will give you the opportunity to fine-tune it. One point you must remember is that your philosophy may change from time to time. When you recognize that it's time to refine your outlook on life, see it as an opportunity to revise it in a way that more accurately reflects you.

Expand Your Horizons

If a genie appeared to you and granted you a single wish to do anything at all with your life, what would you choose? Would you ask for wealth? Fame? Power? Would you want to be a doctor, a ballerina, or an astronaut? Would you wish to live in the woods? In the mountains? By the sea? In the middle of a great bustling city? In a small town?

I have asked this question to any number of people, and most look at me as though I have just asked them to solve a great global problem. But it can be a life-changing question. One day, as you begin your journal entry, ask yourself: If I could do anything with my life, what would it be?

Life Changes

Give it serious thought when you ask yourself what you would do with your life if you could choose anything. At the outset, your response may be, "I like my job. I love my family and they love me." You may even say, "I'm happy where I'm living and I love my house. I don't want to move."

But if you allow yourself to think about the question seriously within the parameters of your philosophy, you may find small weaknesses in your confidence, weaknesses that deserve exploration. After all, if it weren't for explorers, we'd all still live in caves, gather nuts and berries, and hunt to survive. No one would have had the courage to go over the hill to see what lay beyond.

What Do You Want to Be When You Grow Up?

Don't evade the question. Don't put it off. Give it deep thought. Let your mind wander and explore the possibilities in your journal. Suppose you decide that, since you love the outdoors and wildlife, you'd like to be a forest ranger. Begin keeping a log-style journal and consider how it relates to your philosophy of life.

For example, if you have a concern for endangered species, you may find satisfaction in becoming involved with an organization that works to preserve such species. Refer back to Chapter 6, "The Log," which deals extensively with the log journal. It can help you with your research in finding such groups, tracking your research, and eventually getting involved should you take it that far.

Improve the Quality of Your Life

Part of the human condition is always to want to improve our lot in life. The presence or lack of quality of life is a judgment based on what we value. I tend to think we're hard-wired to always want bigger, better, faster, stronger. In short, we human creatures rarely find satisfaction with what we have. Instead, we always have our sights set on something else.

While some may see this as a shortcoming of our species, I see it as one of our strongest traits. The need to achieve more and attain more spurs us on to bigger and better. Life would be incredibly boring if we accepted everything without question or hope of anything better.

When we consider quality of life, it's important to consider four elements in terms of your personal philosophy:

➤ Personal relationships

➤ Professional success

➤ Personal fulfillment

➤ Spiritual and/or character development

Using your journal to explore these aspects of your life enables you to consider each carefully, determine your priorities, and improve the quality of life for yourself as well as for those around you.

Personal Relationships

Statistics show that married people live longer, healthier lives than their unmarried peers. Those who have no meaningful relationships in their lives have more health problems and lower life expectancy. We need close personal relationships to survive.

Your journal is the perfect place to analyze your personal relationships. The question-answer technique is a very straightforward and helpful way to determine just how good your relationships are.

Here are some questions for people with partners to consider:

➤ How happy am I with this person?

➤ Do I love my partner?

➤ Do I feel my partner loves me?

➤ Am I happy to see my partner when he or she walks through the door?

➤ Can I share anything with my partner?

➤ Do we enjoy each other's company?

➤ Do we do special little things for each other?

➤ Do our conversations cover a variety of topics?

➤ How much do I trust my partner?

If you can honestly give positive answers to these questions, I congratulate you on a great relationship with that special person in your life. But as is the case so often in the real world, you will very likely get less than desirable answers for one or two questions. Draw upon your philosophy to determine a course of action for improvement.

Other Than Partners

Friendships come and go as we move from one location to another or change jobs or schools. Some relationships stay intact while others disintegrate despite our best intentions.

Here are some questions you can ask yourself about other close relationships:

➤ How much do I trust this person?

➤ Do we enjoy spending time together?

➤ How much do we have in common?

➤ Do we talk about a variety of subjects?

➤ How often do we see each other?

➤ How much do we laugh together?

Using your personal philosophy for guidance, be brutally honest in your evaluations of your relationships.

Reach Out to Others

Unless you live in a cave, you are well aware that others in your community are in need of some form of help. It may be on a material level such as food and shelter. Perhaps they need medical, dental, or counseling services. Maybe a local foundation sponsors a mentoring program for young people.

If you're not already involved, you should seriously consider contributing some of your time and talents to fulfill these needs. You can use your journal to determine your talents and how best to use them.

Doing Your Homework

If you decide to become involved in any community project, I encourage you to research the availability of programs in your area. Learn what they do, whom they serve, and who funds them. Find out if they have any political or religious ties and what they are.

You should find out all these things to determine how they fit in with your personal philosophy.

Finding Your Talents

Everyone has particular talents. You use them every day in your job, your hobbies, and even your friendships, and you probably already have a very good idea of where yours lie. But you might have some hidden abilities that you never dreamed you possessed. Use your journal to find them.

Start with a list of the talents you know you possess. Let me give you some ideas of what you might consider for your list. Of course, this is just a beginning. Open your mind and consider other possibilities.

➤ I am a detail-oriented person.

➤ I am good with numbers.

➤ I am good at research.

➤ I have good rapport with children.

➤ I am good at fund-raising.

➤ I am good at public relations and dealing with the media.

➤ I have computer skills.

➤ I have a talent for word processing.

➤ I can do accurate data entry.

➤ I have excellent phone skills.

➤ I can teach how to do something step by step.

➤ I can teach an art form (music, drawing, painting, writing, singing, dancing, and so on).

➤ I enjoy working with large groups of people.

➤ I love to work with people one on one.

From the wide variety of items in this list, I'm sure you can find a few that apply to you and then add a few more that pertain to you. In my own case, I know that singing wouldn't apply—anyone who has ever heard me sing would whole-heartedly agree! But I have a talent for standing in front of a group and making a presentation, something that many others would avoid at all costs.

Take a good, critical look at the personal gifts you've listed and then review the information you have about the various community projects.

It's a Match!

The fact that you keep (or are planning to keep) a journal tells me that you are a person of many talents, so I'm sure you'll find several matches. List those that interest you most and to which you think you can contribute the most. Then begin making contact with the people in charge. Offer your time and your talents by doing office work, fundraising, mentoring, fieldwork, or whatever else you think would do the most good. I know of no project that would turn away a well-meaning volunteer with confidence in what she has to offer.

The Write Idea

Some philosophies maintain that whatever you give, whether good or bad, will come back to you threefold. If you adhere to such thinking, then you should do everything in your power to do only good for others in the world.

As you contribute your time and talents to others in the community, the payment you receive in satisfaction and gratitude from those you help more than repays you for your time. In addition, you'll accumulate a wealth of experiences, new friends, new acquaintances, and new things to write about in your journal.

Think of the rich legacy you will leave behind with your contributions. First, your service will help many people; second, the information in your journal will offer an inside view of people helping people.

Achieve!

Success is within your reach. It's up to you whether to grab on to it or not. Never before in our history has there been so much opportunity for so many. But when you talk about achievement, don't limit yourself to the financial aspects. Consider personal growth as a very real way to achieve success.

Put Me in, Coach!

I know you've heard the saying, "Opportunity only knocks once." In many cases this is true, and when it does, you'd better recognize it and be ready to take advantage of it.

It reminds me of the third-string quarterback who has gone to all the practices, knows the plays, and yet sits the bench every game. He's frustrated because he wants to get out there to show his stuff.

Then the first-string quarterback is injured, and the coach puts in the backup quarterback. A few plays later, the second quarterback is taken off the field in a stretcher. The opportunity is now knocking.

The quarterback approaches his coach with that classic plea, "Put me in, Coach!"

Having no other choice, the coach sends him in, and in the fairytale ending, the third-string quarterback leads his team to victory. He was suited up and ready to play. He saw his opportunity and took it.

You, too, can find your opportunities if you know what your goals are and if you possess the knowledge to see it through. Use your journal to set your goals, to put down on paper the opportunities you're looking for, and to help you gather the knowledge you need.

Seizing the Opportunity

Carpe diem, a popular Latin expression meaning "seize the day," wasn't that well-known until the movie *Dead Poet's Society* put it into the popular vernacular. Whether opportunity knocks or you have to create your own inroads, recognize it, write about it, then grab hold of it with both hands.

The Least You Need to Know

➤ You can use your journal to help you formulate a philosophy to live by.

➤ Perspective gives you the insight to know which things in life require attention and action and which you can ignore.

➤ Your journal can help you improve your quality of life by expanding your horizons.

➤ Reaching out to others brings a great deal of satisfaction.

➤ Your journal can help you recognize opportunities and seize them when they present themselves.

233

Chapter 27

You, Your Journal, and Times to Come

In This Chapter

➤ Taking control of your life

➤ Keeping your journal for yourself

➤ Your journal and the outside world

➤ Your journal for generations to come

Keeping a journal has many benefits for you, your community, and generations to come. Consider them all as you write your journal because you can accomplish so much good with what your write. Words do have power.

Never forget the power you have within you to make things happen, not only for yourself but for others. And you transfer that power to the pages of your journal with your choice of words and the concepts they address. Listen to the little voice inside your head that tells you right from wrong and urges you to noble actions. Write about it all in your journal, not only for your own benefit but for others, present and future.

Taking Control

Everyone should keep a journal because everyone has a story to tell. You alone understand the completeness of your joy at the birth of a child or the depth of your sorrow at the loss of a loved one. You alone know the secrets of your heart and the emotions you need to express. With all our responsibilities, too often it seems that life gets out of control, and we have no time for ourselves. You have the ability within to take control. The commitment to keep a journal forces us into making time for ourselves.

It makes us reflect on the day just passed and look at it more objectively. With such objectivity comes many benefits.

Words of Wisdom

"Power can be taken, but not given. The process of the taking is empowerment in itself."

—Gloria Steinem

Practice Makes Perfect

One of the reasons we feel out of control is because we don't know what to expect. We don't have a crystal ball or any other way to reliably predict the future. For that reason, we approach situations tentatively, without the needed confidence to resolve them quickly and in a satisfactory manner.

Whether you have a problem at work, a health problem, or a desire for excellence on a project, writing about it in your journal can be like a simulation for you. Just as pilots hone their skills on computer simulators, you too can run through the scenarios of a situation in your journal so that, in real life, you can succeed.

Getting the Upper Hand

Taking control of a situation goes a long way toward resolving it. Even the appearance of control helps us deal with things in a much more efficient manner. The question then remains: How do you gain the appearance of control?

One technique therapists use with their patients is to have them write the problem down on a piece of paper. Look at it. Read it over and over, then crumple it up and throw it away or burn it. The act of writing it down on a piece of paper and then controlling its fate, its destruction, gives the impression of having power over the issue.

The same idea works when you write about something in your journal. You write it down and then control its fate by closing the pages of your book or computer file.

Try it yourself. Pick an issue that bothers you, that you feel is too big to get a hold of, and write about it. When you have finished, close your book. You'll see how much better you feel about it.

Healthier Living

In addition to gaining control over the circumstances of your life, a journal helps you live a healthier life. If you have a medical condition, writing about it can help you manage pain and other symptoms, in many cases allowing patients to decrease medication. Write about your condition and why it bothers you. Describe all the other things in life that grate on your nerves. You should soon see some improvement in how you feel.

Clinical tests have shown that, if you already enjoy good health, keeping a journal boosts your immune system, making it easier for you to maintain your health. Use your journal to plan and record diet and exercise. Write about the things that bother you and take control.

Striving for Excellence

Many of us view perfection as the holy grail, but realistically, we know we can never achieve that. We're human and not the stuff of gods. No matter how hard we try, there will always be a comma out of place or something we wish we had included.

Once again, your journal comes to the rescue as a way for you to achieve excellence, a goal you can reach. Write about what you want to do, make your plans to get there, and then track your progress. It's a matter of feeling in control and then acting on it in a confident way.

A Way to Practice

Just as pilots use a simulator, your journal becomes a way for you to make a dry run through a variety of situations. Writing about it from a variety of angles enables you to see different ways to approach a problem or project. With such a perspective, you can take on the world with a confidence born of knowledge, take control, and succeed.

Words of Wisdom

"Excellence encourages one about life generally; it shows the spiritual wealth of the world."

—George Eliot

A Better Person

One of the other benefits of keeping a journal is personal growth. By taking the time to write about your life, your feelings, your plans, and the kind of person you wish to become, you can achieve. Perhaps you want to explore and expand your ethics. Maybe you want to become a more spiritual person. Your journal stands ready and waiting to help you get there.

Words of Wisdom

"The sensual and spiritual are linked together by a mysterious bond, sensed by our emotions, though hidden from our eyes."

—Karl Wilhelm Von Humboldt

Going Through a Growth Spurt

Take the opportunity a journal gives you to grow spiritually. Take the time to think about yourself and how you can improve. Look at yourself spiritually and address ways to rearrange your priorities so that material things hold less importance in your life. Determine how you can grow closer to the divine in your life.

Look to your soul, feel it, listen to it, and write what it tells you. You know it's there. It warns you when something isn't right, and it warms you when you've done something wonderful.

Explore Your Emotions

Along with your spirituality, you should use your journal to examine your emotions. Do you value the positive emotions of love, thoughtfulness, and consideration more than the negative feelings of anger, frustration, and fear? Do you show how you feel or keep it bottled up inside? Think about yourself and determine whether you're a person who smiles easily. Do you tell the people in your life that you care about them or keep your love hidden?

Use your journal to help you become more expressive, to give and get love from others, or to let everyone know you're angry in an appropriate way. Being able to laugh and cry and express emotions is one of the things that makes us human. Teach yourself to let your humanity come through at every opportunity, and you will see a difference in your life.

Your Journal and the Outside World

None of us operates in a vacuum. Each of us touches myriad other lives, just as we react to so many others. We cannot go about our lives minding our own business as though the rest of the world doesn't matter. To put it as plainly and as simply as I can, the rest of the world does matter.

Around the corner or around the world, whether you realize it or not, the events that directly touch other people's lives have some affect on you as well. Keep a journal. Remain aware. Then take appropriate action to touch someone's life.

Words of Wisdom

"It is very difficult to be wholly joyous or wholly sad on this earth. The comic, when it is human, soon takes upon itself a face of pain; and some of our griefs ... have their source in weaknesses which must be recognized with smiling compassion as the common inheritance of us all."

—Joseph Conrad

Words of Wisdom

"No man is an island entire of itself; every man is part of the main ... Any man's death diminishes me because I am involved in mankind, and therefore never send to know for whom the bell tolls; it tolls for thee."

—John Donne

Your Community

Journal keeping can be solitary or global. You can keep your words locked within the pages of your book or computer file, or you can share them with the world. What you think matters. What you say can affect others. Remember, words have power.

Use your journal to write about things that happen in the world around you. When disaster strikes, describe it, make a list of ways you can help, and then do it. When you see an injustice, record it, tell how you feel about it, and then try to figure out a way to make it right. Then describe your efforts in your diary as well as the results.

You Can Make a Difference

One life makes a difference, as does one pair of helping hands. If you touch one other person in a positive way with your efforts, it will all be worthwhile. Joining a service organization or volunteering for a community project makes a difference in a community as well as an individual's life.

Write about your experiences in your journal and how they made you feel. You'll notice that the actions that give the most direct help to others provide you with the warmest, most satisfying feelings.

Describe what in particular gratified you and how it made you a better person. And, at the end of your life, what will matter most to you? That you accumulated great wealth or that many people loved you?

Words of Wisdom

"That best portion of a good
    man's life;
His little, nameless, unremem-
    bered acts
Of kindness and of love."

—William Wordsworth

In Your Footsteps

Although you as well as society can gain many benefits from your journaling, don't forget about the good your journals can do in the future. Throughout a lifetime, you will gain knowledge and understanding of everything around you. Writing about it through your own perceptions will leave a valuable legacy to those who follow in your footsteps.

As you write in your journal, first and foremost keep yourself in mind. A journal is, after all, primarily for your benefit. However, don't forget about those who will come after you.

Your Descendants

Grandchildren and great-grandchildren eventually become curious about those who came before them. They begin to ask questions about past generations and research their family history. For the most part, they construct a family tree with names, dates, and little else.

They know very little or nothing about the people whose names they write on the branches, but think about how they would feel if they suddenly came upon your diaries. I can almost picture them, lovingly and with reverence opening the pages of the book that holds your words.

You suddenly come alive as your words flow into them. Your name changes from a dry and lifeless piece of data to a real live human being of flesh and blood. Don't tell me that you wouldn't want to leave such a gift behind. Your words can teach and show the way to a new generation. What you have to say matters now, and it can have an impact in the future as well.

For Scholars

Historians and genealogists also can benefit from your words. Think what a treasure your diaries would be to someone researching the time in which you lived. If you write about yourself as well as the world around you, you can give an account of world events as you experienced them and as you perceived them.

Did you write about the fall of the Berlin Wall? How did that make you feel? How did you react? Don't you think historians would want to know how people felt about that historic event?

Where were you on the day President John F. Kennedy was assassinated or the day the space shuttle *Challenger* exploded? I'll bet you know exactly where you were, what you were doing, whom you were with, and how you reacted. Did you write about it? If not, it's still not too late.

My Broken Record

If it sounds as if I've said all this before, it's because I have. But I feel it is crucial to remind you about the importance of keeping a journal for your own benefit as well as for others. You have a responsibility to yourself as well as to the future to keep a journal. One life does matter. One person's words have impact. A single life is a microcosm of the human experience, and your journal can tell that story from your unique point of view.

If you already keep a journal, perhaps I've given you some ideas to expand your use of this tool and have shown you how to derive additional benefits from it. If you were thinking about keeping a journal, maybe I've given you some powerful reasons to begin.

In either case, I hope you have found at least some of what you were looking for about journals, that I have answered some of your questions, given you some ideas, and in the end, helped you improve your quality of life.

If you're still not convinced about the importance of keeping a journal, then let me leave you with one thought to ponder: You have a great deal of power to achieve your goals and to succeed at anything you wish. The power, born of stardust and hope, lies within you and clamors for expression. Don't ignore it.

The Least You Need to Know

➤ Keeping a journal enables you to take control of your life and situations you face.

➤ A journal can assist you in becoming a better person.

➤ Your journal can help you grow spiritually and emotionally.

➤ When you write in your journal on a regular basis, you can come to realize all the wonderful things you have in your life.

➤ Your journal can become a valuable historical record for your descendants as well as historians.

➤ You have the power within you to succeed.

241

Internet Sites for Journal Keepers

About.com

journals.about.com/gi/dynamic/offsite.htm?site=http://soulfulliving.com/
writingindark.htm

This Web site features Kathleen Adams and offers information about dream interpretation, getting the most from your dreams, and keeping track of them in your dream journal.

Aisling-Dream Interpretation Tutorial

www.avcweb.com/dreams/tutorial.htm#tutorialbasics

The site gives suggestions on dream interpretation, and how dreams relate to spirituality.

Center for Autobiographic Studies

storyhelp.com/

Look to this site for a wealth of information, resources, and even workshops for the journaler as well as ideas for starting a journaling or memoir writing group in your own neighborhood.

The Center for Journal Therapy

www.journaltherapy.com/

Another Kathleen Adams Web site that discusses the variety of journals, their benefits, as well as offering software and other products.

Conversations Within

www.journal-writing.com/

If you want coaching, information, and exercises for your journal, check out this site.

Diaries and Journals on the Internet
worldimage.com/diaries/index.html

If you want an online site that invites you to submit your own diary entries as well as read others, spend a few minutes online at this address.

EGroups
www.egroups.com/dir/Arts/Writing/Online_Journals

Check out this site for online journals as well as a list of resources for diarists and writers and an online newsletter.

Journal/Diary/Writing Questions
web.cetlink.net/~papabear/Journal/Question.html

This site offers suggested questions for every day of the year for you to consider when you write in your journal.

The Journal Store
www.thejournalstore.com/

If you want to know what's available for journalers, look here for an online cornucopia of books, software, pens, and papers.

Journals Home Page
www.journals.about.com/arts/writepub/journals/mbody.htm

This is a complete site of information for journalers of all ages, from types of journals and online journals, to writing hints and resources.

Keeping a Journal
www.wofford.edu/studyabroad/journal.htm

This site offers thoughts on journals, with a bibliography as well as journal assignments.

Keeping a Garden Journal
www.arnprior.com/kidsgarden/planning/journal.htm

Targeted primarily toward children, this Web site makes practical suggestions on using a journal to plan, cultivate, and harvest a garden.

Keeping a Reflective Journal
west.pima.edu/~acc/csl/Journal.htm

This page of the Center for Service Learning provides suggestions for keeping a reflective journal as a tool in the learning process.

Live Your Dream
www.joycechapman.com/

Dedicated to making your dreams come true, this site offers coaching, links, and online journaling.

National Journal Network
www.geocities.com/SoHo/9993/

This online journaling site has the added features of monthly writing ideas, links, and a chat room.

New Life Stories
www.newlifestories.com/

Check this site out for a newsletter, resources, bookchat, quotations, and writing prompts.

Personal Journaling
writersdigest.com/journaling

A site sponsored by "Personal Journaling," it offers information about the variety of journals as well as how to keep your creativity up.

Progoff Intensive Journal Program
www.intensivejournal.org/

This site gives information about the Intensive Journal Method developed by Dr. Ira Progoff, the father of modern journaling, offers education, workshops, tapes, articles, all on the subject of journaling.

Programs for Home and Office
www.secureaction.com/memoirs

An easy to use site, it has software and sample programs for journalers and writers.

The Veech Journal Pages
www.nzdances.co.nz/journal/index.html#Line

An online journaling site that also offers chat rooms and other journal information.

Whole Heart
www.whole-heart.com/

Take a few minutes at this site for the online resources, motivation, and support for your journaling habit as well as online workshops and newsletters.

Wordshop—Write from the Heart
intotem.buffnet.net/mhw/Writing_Assignments.html

This site offers excellent ideas for writing assignments for your journal.

Writing the Journey—Online Journal-Writing Workshop
www.writingthejourney.com/

An online journaling workshop with lots of good advice.

Index

Symbols

9¹/₂ Mystics: The Kabbala Today (Weiner, Wiesel, and Steinsaltz), 103
365 Days of Spiritual Growth (Miller), 101

A

About.com Web site, 243
active voice, 191
  editing entries, 192-193
  examples, 193
  rules of thumb, 194
  versus passive voice, 191-192
adjectives, 194-196
adverbs, 195-196
Aisling-Dream Interpretation Tutorial Web site, 243
anger, expressing, 78-79
anniversaries, 148-149
anxiety, facing, 79
autobiographies (versus historical journals), 126-127
Autobiography (Franklin), 46
automatic writing exercise (cathartic journals), 71
awards (special journal topics), 151

B

babies (special journal topics), 145-147
baggage, emotional, 64, 70-71
  automatic writing exercise, 71
  broken record exercise, 70-71
  healing process, 64-65
  "holding on," 65
  incomplete sentences exercise, 68-70
  venting, 65-68
benefits, 12, 18, 140-141. *See also* purposes
  adults, 15
  children, 12-14
  self-awareness and healing, 15-16
  sounding board, 39
  teenagers, 14-15
binders, 19
Biorhythms: A Step-by-Step Guide (West), 29
birthday journals, 148
body-mind connection. *See* mind-body connection
books
  9¹/₂ Mystics: The Kabbala Today (Weiner, Wiesel, and Steinsaltz), 103
  365 Days of Spiritual Growth (Miller), 101
  Autobiography (Franklin), 46
  Biorhythms: A Step-by-Step Guide (West), 29
  Complete Idiot's Guide to Awakening Your Spirituality, The (Robinson), 104
  Confessions (St. Augustine of Hippo), 5
  Diary of Samuel Pepys, The, 6
  Essential Spirituality: The 7 Central Practices to Awaken Heart and Mind (Walsh), 104
  Grief Observed, A (Lewis), 65
  Healing and the Mind (Moyers), 57
  Makura no Sōshi/The Pillow Book of Sei Shōnagon, 6
  Mind on Fire: A Faith for the Skeptical and Indifferent (Pascal), 7
  Spirituality of Imperfection: Storytelling and the Journey to Wholeness, The (Kurtz and Ketcham), 105
  Writing to Access the Power of the Unconscious and Evoke Creative Ability (Progoff), 8
broken record exercise (cathartic journals), 70-71

C

cars, 173

catch-all journals, 220

cathartic journals, 34-35

 emotional baggage, 64

  healing process, 64-65

  "holding on," 65

 exercises, 70-71

  automatic writing, 71

  broken record, 70-71

  incomplete sentences, 68-70

 venting, 65-68

 versus unsent letters, 73-74

Center for Autobiographic Studies Web site, 243

Center for Journal Therapy Web site, 243

character development, 96-98

characters, 179-181

 secondary, 182-183

 "show don't tell," 183

 you as the main character, 181-182

  descriptions, 181

  photographs, 182

chat rooms, 210

children

 growing up, 13-14

 recording quotes, 153-154

 starting a journal, 12-13

college graduations (special journal topics), 149

comic strips (as journal entries), 157

community involvement, 231

 identifying contributable talents, 231-232

 matching skills with need, 232

 researching need, 231

Complete Idiot's Guide to Awakening Your Spirituality, The (Robinson), 104

computers, 199, 206

 accessories, 200-201

  printers, 200-201

  scanners, 201

 composing entries, 204-205

 desktops, 199-200

 editing entries, 205-206

 Internet journaling, 207-211

  exchanging, 22

  interacting with other journalers, 209-210

  newsgroups, 210-211

 laptops, 200

 programs, 201

  filing, 202

  software, 203-204

  word-processing, 201-204

 starting out, 22-23

 versus pen and paper, 21-23

Confessions (St. Augustine of Hippo), 5-6

connection, mind-body, 55

 faith, 56

 placebo effect, 56-57

contemplation, 105

control, gaining, 235-236

control step (theme journals), 90

Conversations Within Web sites, 243

conversations. *See* dialogue

creative outlets, 155

 comic strips, 157

 drawings, 156

 humor, 156-157

 jokes, 157

 music, 155-156

 poetry, 156

D

daily writing

 benefits, 31

 making time, 26-30

 selecting a place to write, 30-31

death, 160-163

decision-making, 85

descriptions (sensory), 187-188

desktop computers, 199-200

dialogue, 185-186

 accuracy, 186

 format, 186-187

Diaries and Journals on the Internet Web site, 244

Diary of Samuel Pepys, The, 6

digital journaling. *See* computers

divorce, 161

drawings, 156

dream journals, 36

 daydreams, 122

  considering possibilities, 122

  recording fantasies, 122

  visualization, 122-123

 documenting dreams, 117

 finding patterns, 121

 interpretations, 117-121

  common interpretations, 118

  maintaining perspective, 120-121

 making dreams come true, 123

 nature of dreams, 116-117

 steps for understanding dreams, 118

  connecting with reality, 119

  deciding whether to act, 119

W-Z

Your Journal

Your Journal

Your Journal

Your Journal

Your Journal

Your Journal

Your Journal

Your Journal

Your Journal

Your Journal